THE ENIGMA OF
the knights templar

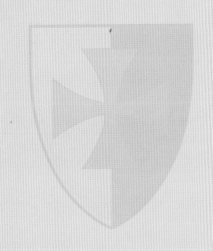

THE ENIGMA OF

the knights templar

THEIR HISTORY AND MYSTICAL CONNECTIONS

MARILYN HOPKINS

Published by The Disinformation Company Ltd.
163 Third Avenue, Suite 108
New York, NY 10003
Tel.: +1.212.691.1605
Fax: +1.212.691.1606
www.disinfo.com

Library of Congress Control Number: 2006925223

ISBN-10: 1-932857-44-3
ISBN-13: 978-1-932857-44-3
Printed in China

10 9 8 7 6 5 4 3 2 1

This book was conceived, designed, and produced
by Ixos, an imprint of Ivy Press
The Old Candlemakers, West Street,
Lewes, East Sussex BN7 2NZ, U.K.
www.ivy-group.co.uk

Publisher: David Alexander
Creative Director: Peter Bridgewater
Art Director: Sarah Howerd and Kevin Knight
Editorial Director: Caroline Earle
Senior Project Editor: Hazel Songhurst
Designer: Nicola Liddiard
Project Designer: Joanna Clinch
Picture Researcher: Shelley Noronha

Distributed in the U.S.A. and Canada by:
Consortium Book Sales and Distribution
1045 Westgate Drive, Suite 90
St Paul, MN 55114
Toll Free: +1.800.283.3572
Local: +1.651.221.9035
Fax: +1.651.221.0124
www.cbsd.com

contents

introduction

THE KNIGHTS TEMPLAR STIMULATED TRANSFORMATIVE CHANGE THROUGHOUT EUROPE. AFTER TWO CENTURIES THEY WERE ARRESTED, TORTURED, AND DISBANDED. THEIR CONTROVERSIAL ORIGINS, TRUE BELIEFS, AND THE SUDDEN DISAPPEARANCE OF THEIR VAST TREASURE, REMAIN SHROUDED IN MYSTERY.

The foundation of the medieval Order of the Knights Templar bears all the hallmarks of a massive conspiracy. The generally accepted date for the foundation is 1118, although it may in fact have been several years earlier, and a review of the records of the founding members reveals that the leaders were all related either by blood or by marriage to Count Hughes I of Champagne in France.

Despite their declared task of guarding the main pilgrimage routes between the ancient port of Jaffa on the coast of Palestine to Jerusalem, the founding knights spent the first nine years of the order's existence excavating beneath their quarters in what they believed to have been the stables of the Temple of Solomon. This immediately raises some intriguing questions: What were they looking for? How did they know where to dig? And what, if anything, did they find?

When these mysterious excavations were completed, the founding members returned to Europe. The order grew rapidly, attracting substantial donations of land and property in Europe, and soon attained incredible power and influence. In his bull of 1138, Pope Innocent II made the order answerable to the pope alone, which freed the knights from interference from any other authority, thus making them the most independent religious order in the Christian world. The Knights Templar are renowned for creating the first standing army since the days of the Roman Empire, for the sole purpose of fighting the Muslims in the Holy Land.

The Templars were not merely the first order of warrior-monks but they also laid the foundations for the first truly international banking system, ultimately paving the way for the rise of modern capitalism. By the time of their suppression, their vast holdings of over 9,000 properties (estates or tracts of land), spanned all of Europe with their principal properties in France. These estates had one function above all others, to provide the funds to sustain the wars in the Holy Land.

The order's fall from grace was sudden, dramatic, and brutal. On Friday October 13, 1307, most of the knights in France were arrested, including the Grand Master, Jacques de Molay. However, word had leaked of their impending doom, and the 18 ships that had borne the Grand Master and his entourage to France had disappeared from the port of La Rochelle on the French Atlantic coast. The knights arrested in France were handed over to the tender mercies of the Inquisition; elsewhere the situation varied. Spain needed them to help fight against the Moors who had ruled over much of the Iberian Peninsula since the early eighth century; in Portugal they changed their name to the Order of the Knights of Christ; many knights in the Baltic States joined the Teutonic Knights; and those in Lombardy, northern Italy, used their skills to strengthen the emergent banking system. Many fled to Scotland, where the whole country had been excommunicated, making it the one place where the knights were completely safe.

But what of the Templar treasure? By the time the king's men entered the treasury of the Paris Temple, in France, the treasure had vanished without trace. The Temple, used as a safe deposit for the royal income, was the treasury of the order in France and the amount of coinage held there would have been enormous.

According to later French Freemasonic ritual, most of the treasure had been shipped to Scotland. Another part is reputed to have been smuggled north to what is now Belgium.

It may well be that some of the theories expressed in this book will be challenging to some readers; and it is true that many do not follow the conventional historical interpretation of the facts. I have, however, researched the Knights Templar over a long period, and together with a number of eminent contemporary historians (some of these are listed in the bibliography), have reached the conclusions that you will find in this book.

History, however, rarely respects the needs of the chronicler, and to really understand the complex web of activity of the Knights Templar we will have to weave back and forth in time, tracing each strand in turn, and to gain an insight into the real reasons for the foundation of the order, first examine the conflicts that lie at the heart of the development of Christianity and its origins in Biblical Israel.

A TEMPLAR IN CHAIN MAIL DISPLAYING THE CROIX PATTÉE (AN EIGHT-POINTED TEMPLAR CROSS), CARRYING A LANCE, AND BEARING A POMMEL SWORD. BEHIND HIM IS HIS WARHORSE OR *DESTRIER*.

the templar heritage

THE EVENTS LEADING TO THE FORMATION OF THE ORDER OF THE KNIGHTS TEMPLAR HAVE THEIR REAL ORIGINS AT THE TIME OF JESUS AND CONTINUE UNTIL THE ERA OF THE CRUSADES, WHEN THE CHRISTIAN ARMIES FOUGHT THE SARACENS FOR CONTROL OF THE HOLY LAND.

It is difficult for many Christians today to accept that Christianity was founded not so much on the teachings of Jesus but more on the thinking of Saul of Tarsus, or St. Paul. After Paul's conversion on the road to Damascus in the mid-30s CE and following three years spent in Arabia, Paul went to Jerusalem and joined James the Just, the first Bishop of Jerusalem and the brother of Jesus, and his followers to learn "the Way," as taught by Jesus. Following this he undertook a series of prolonged evangelical journeys preaching to the gentiles (non-Jews) in some of the most important cities of the eastern Mediterranean.

It is very clear in the New Testament and other sources that there were fundamental differences between "the Way" of the Essenes as it was interpreted by James and the original disciples, and the version promulgated by Paul, who, according to his own letters, had never met the living Jesus. The Essenes were a group of ultra-orthodox Jews who followed an initiatory path known as "the Way." They sprang from an earlier esoteric branch of Judaism, known as the Theraputae, which practiced mainly in the vicinity of Alexandria in Egypt. The original followers of Jesus, his disciples, and members of his immediate family, who became known as the Ebionites, were dedicated to the Torah, the sacred body of Law that was the basis of their covenant with God. They maintained the prohibition against mixing with gentiles, kept strictly to the dietary laws, and tried to create an "elite within the elite of Israel" in preparation for the victory of the people of the light over the powers of darkness that would come in the Last Days. Yet, according to Paul, the old covenant, or Berit, and its laws, were no longer applicable. The covenant made between God and Abraham stated that if the people kept the Law as enshrined in the Torah, Abraham would be the father of many nations and his descendants would become a light unto the gentiles. Paul refuted this absolutely and claimed that all that was needed for salvation was faith, and faith alone. Paul was also responsible for the deification of Jesus, an idea that outraged Jesus' original followers and all other Jews. Furthermore, he taught that Jesus had been a form of sacrificial lamb who had "died for our sins," in contradiction to the Jewish law that forbade human sacrifice in any form.

Paul was rejected by the followers of Jesus in Jerusalem, and his evangelical mission was steadily losing ground to those evangelists who carried written accreditation from James. Indeed, according to the Catholic historian Paul Johnson, if it hadn't been for the destruction of Jerusalem in 70 CE, Paul's efforts might have been forgotten altogether and would not even have been a footnote in Jewish history.

THE CITY OF JERUSALEM WAS THE SPIRITUAL CENTER FOR JEWS, CHRISTIANS, AND MUSLIMS THROUGHOUT THE TEMPLAR PERIOD.

THE RISE OF THE CHRISTIAN CHURCH

In the Acts of the Apostles, James and the original followers of Jesus are described as the "first church in Jerusalem." However, the beliefs of the other early "Christians," founded as they were on the teaching of St. Paul who preached that Jesus was divine, differed very markedly indeed from the original initiatory teachings of Jesus. Yet despite this, the traditional structure of the early Church was clearly founded on Essene practice. The early Church used a book called the *Didache*, or the teaching of the Lord, whose regulations were used by the emerging Christian communities: the similarities between the *Didache* and the Essene Community

Rule found among the Dead Sea Scrolls are startling, which is especially strange when viewed in the light of the Church's attempts to set the date of the latter in a much earlier era.

The repercussions of the failure of the Jewish revolt against Roman rule that ended in 70 CE were so profound that they changed the course of history in ways that are still felt to this day. The Jewish people in particular paid a high price with the destruction of the Temple and the city of Jerusalem. Jews were prohibited by the Romans from inhabiting the city and the emperor issued orders that all those claiming descent from the House of David were to be executed on sight.

This was a traumatic time across the entire Holy Land. It was a period that saw the Diaspora, the scattering of the Jewish people beyond the boundaries of Israel and amongst other people and nations as far afield to what is now Western Europe. Those that remained were forced to discard their fervent nationalism and anti-Roman stance, and to keep their beliefs secret in order to preserve their teachings and avoid persecution. This dispersion included the followers of Jesus in Jerusalem, and cleared the way for the Pauline Christians to denationalize Jesus and recast him as a "savior god."

The historian Paul Johnson claims that "Christianity began in confusion, controversy, and Schism and so it continued. A dominant orthodox church, with a recognizable ecclesiastical structure, emerged only very gradually ... As with all such struggles, it was not particularly edifying." By the middle of the second century the congregation in Rome began to take precedence over other Christian groups, but it took a further

two centuries for the chaos of the early years to be turned into any real semblance of order.

CONSTANTINE THE GREAT

Constantine the Great became emperor of the Roman Empire after a civil war that ended with his victory at the battle of the Milvian Bridge in 314 CE. He passed the *Edict of Milan* shortly afterward, giving the Christian Church religious freedom, banning its persecution, and guaranteeing its property rights. To commemorate the victory, Constantine erected a triumphal arch in Rome inscribed with the cross of Christ, even though he was not a Christian but a follower of Sol Invictus, the god of the Mithraic sun-worshipping cult. This had its origins in Zoroastrianism, a religion that arose in Persia (modern Iran). However, when the emperor was seen to favor the new religion many of his followers became Christians as an act of political advantage. Despite this, Christianity did not become the officially preferred state religion until near the end of the fourth century.

Constantine divided the empire into two parts: Rome became the capital of the Western Empire while Constantinople, named after himself, became the capital of the Eastern Empire. His toleration of Christianity was a calculated political act. Christians were disciplined and

ABOVE: A FRAGMENT OF THE COPPER SCROLL DISCOVERED AMONG THE DEAD SEA SCROLLS THAT MENTION THE TREASURE BENEATH THE TEMPLE OF SOLOMON.

RIGHT: EMPEROR CONSTANTINE VALUED THE STATE ABOVE ALL ELSE. HE USED THE CHRISTIAN RELIGION TO FURTHER HIS POLITICAL AMBITIONS.

law-abiding, and he wished to use their beliefs to heal the bitter rift that the civil war had caused throughout the empire. This amalgamation of religious and secular power appeared to create a Church/state alliance that he hoped would unify the empire.

However, the emergent Christian Church was itself plagued by doctrinal argument, intolerance, and vituperative theological debate. This mainly focussed on the disputed nature of Jesus—was he a man or was he God? Now, the empire was in danger of being torn apart by the disunity within the Church. For Emperor Constantine the interests of the state came first, for he valued unity, order, and stability far above religious dogma. To impose his will on the squabbling clerics he convened the first ecumenical council of the Church at Nicea (now Iznik in Turkey) in 325.

THE COUNCIL OF NICEA

The most important issue at the council was the argument between the followers of Arius, who believed that Jesus was a divinely inspired man, and those of Paul, who believed he was God incarnate. The conclusion condemned the teachings of Arius as heretical, and it was decreed that any statement or fact that contradicted or devalued Church teaching was also heretical and was to be punished by exile, by confiscation of property, or death.

By the time of Emperor Theodosius in the fifth century, the number of specific laws against heresy, the first of which had been promulgated in the 380s, had multiplied until there were over 100 statutes aimed at heretics.

The council of Nicea had vowed to excommunicate anyone who did not accept the doctrine that Jesus was divine. This ruling set a precedent for the repression to come in the centuries that followed.

THE SPREAD OF CHRISTIANITY

By the end of the fifth century, after the fall of the Roman Empire in the West, the Church had taken on many of the functions previously undertaken by the state. In the minds of the general populace the two became indistinguishable: to be a Roman was to be a Christian and vice versa.

The Church had gained a monopoly on everything sacred in Western Europe by the mid-sixth century. It controlled all religious matters and stultified the search for knowledge

and truth in the secular world for centuries. Pope Gregory "the Great" became the *de facto* ruler of Italy in the latter half of the sixth century for, in the absence of any secular authority, he raised troops, appointed generals, and made treaties. He was exceedingly zealous wherever the well-being of the Church was concerned, initiating the idea of enforced celibacy for the clergy and instigating a strict code for the election of bishops. Gregory the Great was the first pope who was also a monk.

THE FIRST HOLY ROMAN EMPEROR

On Christmas Day 800, the king of the Franks, Charles Augustus, who claimed succession from the biblical kings of Israel, was crowned emperor by Pope Leo III. No emperor had reigned in Rome for the previous 324 years. Charles the Great, or Charlemagne, thus became the first Holy

Roman Emperor, a statesman whose military prowess and commercial shrewdness led to an ever-expanding realm. He established an empire that spanned the entire heartland of Western Europe from the River Danube to the Pyrenees and from Rome to the North Sea. He was renowned for his tolerance toward the Jews, whose protection was assured under his reign, for Charlemagne was aware that the Jews were the key to success in international trade, so he and his nobles encouraged Jewish immigration into the empire as a matter of state policy. Prior to his coronation Europe was an area of tribal settlement with largely nonexistent frontiers.

THE CORONATION OF CHARLEMAGNE, THE FIRST HOLY ROMAN EMPEROR. CHARLEMAGNE'S COURT AT AIX-LA-CHAPELLE BECAME THE CENTER OF A CULTURAL REBIRTH IN EUROPE.

THE RISE OF ISLAM

The prophet Muhammad received a series of revelations in the early seventh century CE. He had grown up in an area heavily influenced by a large Jewish population and an even larger Christian community. The prevailing Christianity was not that as preached by St. Paul, but Monophysite, a doctrine held by early Coptic, or Syrian, Christians that Jesus was a man who had been divinely inspired.

Muhammad believed himself to be a prophet in the tradition of Abraham, Moses, Elijah, John the Baptist, and Jesus. Indeed, he claimed to be the last of the divine messengers who had all testified to the same religion of "the one true God." Muhammad believed that he had been called upon to restore true monotheism, which had existed since ancient times, and not to found a new religion. The Prophet's authority ended the incessant feuding of the Arab

tribes and gave them a sense of national and religious identity akin to that of the Byzantine Christians of the Eastern Roman Empire and the Jews. Now the Arab peoples had their own book of Divine Revelation and a religion of obedience and service to God.

Islam initiated an era of considerable political stability for the Arab people and was, from the outset, remarkably tolerant of other faiths, especially "the people of the book," namely Christians and Jews. Muhammad made the nomadic tribes of Arabia into a nation that went on to create an immense empire and found a great civilization.

In 634, the armies of Islam conquered Jerusalem, where the Jews welcomed the invaders, preferring their tolerant religious attitude to the persecution directed at them by the Christians. Alexandria capitulated in 646, and by 714, the Arab armies had reached Central Asia and northern India in the East and had overrun the Iberian Peninsula in the West.

Their attempt to invade France in 732 failed, however, and they were driven back to Spain. Nonetheless, Christian pilgrims were free to visit the Holy Land, and in Jerusalem the Church of the Holy Sepulchre was permitted to remain in Christian hands.

EAST VERSUS WEST

The Christian leaders were constantly aware of the threat of Islam but spent most of their time fighting each other. The situation was much the same in the East, where violence was endemic as the succession of each caliph (head of Islam) gave rise to civil war. The main difference between the warring factions in the East and the West was that the caliph had the power of a unified state, whereas the West had many different principalities which, after the death of Charlemagne, were never reunited under one rule.

14

There was a great deal of rivalry between the Western Christians in Rome and the Byzantine Greeks, who were held in contempt by the Roman Church. However, when it came to the conflict between the Byzantine Christians and Islam, Rome tended to support their coreligionists. In 1071, the Byzantine Christians came up against an army of Seljuk Turks. The Byzantines were defeated and the emperor was taken captive. By 1081 the Turks had swept across Asia Minor to within a 100 miles of Constantinople. The Byzantines appealed to their fellow Christians in the West for aid, and in 1085, a small contingent of knights was sent to Constantinople. In 1089, the new pope, Urban II, raised the ban of excommunication upon Emperor Alexius of Byzantium. This encouraged the emperor to seek aid from the Roman Church in his fight against the Turks, and in 1096, the pope called for the First Crusade against Islam.

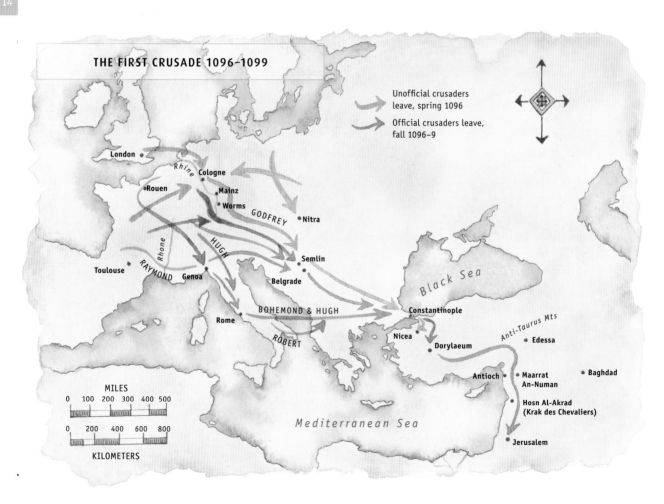

THE FIRST CRUSADE 1096–1099

Unofficial crusaders leave, spring 1096

Official crusaders leave, fall 1096–9

London

Rhine · Cologne

Rouen · · Mainz · Worms · GODFREY · Nitra

HUGH

Rhone

RAYMOND · Genoa · Semlin

Toulouse · · Belgrade

Black Sea

BOHEMOND & HUGH · Constantinople

Rome

Nicea · Anti-Taurus Mts

ROBERT · Dorylaeum · · Edessa

Antioch · · Maarrat An-Numan · · Baghdad

Hosn Al-Akrad (Krak des Chevaliers)

Mediterranean Sea

· Jerusalem

MILES
0 100 200 300 400 500

0 200 400 600 800
KILOMETERS

THE FIRST CRUSADE

In 1097, the crusading army crossed the Bosphorus into Anatolia and was attacked outside Nicea by the Turks. The Turkish sultan was defeated, and the crusading army marched on and gained a second victory at Dorylaeum, near modern Eskisehir in central-west Turkey. Eventually the crusaders laid siege to the Christian city of Antioch, which had been garrisoned by Turks for the previous 12 years. The crusading army took the town and remained there through the heat of the summer. They set out on the long and arduous march to Jerusalem on January 13, 1099, and arrived before the walls of the Holy City on June 7. The assault on Jerusalem began on July 13, and the crusaders gained entry the following day.

When the city fell, the Christian army slaughtered the inhabitants with no quarter given for age or sex with the exception of a few Muslims who, having been given safe conduct by Count Raymond IV of Toulouse, escaped with their lives in exchange for the city's treasure. The Jews fled to their synagogue, but the crusaders set fire to it, burning them alive. One contemporary chronicler described how "in the portico of Solomon and in his Temple, our men rode in the blood of Saracens up to the knees of their horses."

On July 17, Mass was celebrated and thanks given for the victory. By 1100, most of the crusaders had returned to Europe, leaving a small force of 300 knights and 300 foot soldiers to protect their conquests.

the order of the temple

THE REX DEUS FAMILIES' ACTIVITIES BECAME PUBLIC WITH THE FOUNDATION OF
THE KNIGHTS TEMPLAR. ALL THE FOUNDING MEMBERS WERE PART OF THIS GROUP,
RELATED BY BLOOD OR MARRIAGE, WITH THE CHURCHMAN BERNARD OF CLAIRVAUX
INSTRUMENTAL IN THEIR FORMATION.

little-known esoteric legend in Europe recounts the history of the families who call themselves Rex Deus, and who claim to trace their descent from the 24 hereditary high priests of the Temple of Jerusalem, or the ma'madot. Within Rex Deus were an even more select group known as the Desposyni, who are alleged to be the direct descendants of Jesus. Rex Deus members passed on certain secret teachings from father to son or daughter, down through the generations. Their traditions focussed on an alternative view of Jesus and his teaching and preserved and transmitted these beliefs within the group in secret for over 1,000 years, awaiting the day when it might be safe to disseminate them more widely among the general public. Outwardly, they practiced the prevailing religion of their country while secretly preserving the true initiatory teaching that Jesus had received from John the Baptist and later transmitted to John the Divine and certain of the original disciples, the founders of the Rex Deus families. Thus essential spiritual truths were passed down from master to pupil until, in the twelfth century, they decided that the time was right to act publicly and in unison for the first time

REX DEUS DISAPPEAR FROM VIEW

The next account we have of the Rex Deus families comes from the fourth century when, according to Rex Deus tradition, the body of the Messiah was reburied under the Temple Mount, the one place no one would dream of looking. Any form of human or animal burial on that site was forbidden, as the Temple Mount was deemed to be sacred ground and inviolable. Interestingly, the only Christian cathedral where there are no interments is that of Chartres in France, which was influenced by Rex Deus involvement and whose building was largely financed by the Templars.

From the time of the fall of the Roman Empire, it is difficult to trace the Rex Deus families until the time of

Charlemagne, who appointed many of them to positions of power throughout Europe, after which their individual achievements and complex marital alliances become a matter of record. Indeed, it is only in the years immediately prior to the time that Hughes de Payen became one of the founders of the Order of the Knights Templar, some three centuries after Charlemagne, that their collective actions began to come into the open.

AREAS OF REX DEUS INFLUENCE IN EUROPE: 11TH–15TH CENTURIES

❶	BARONY OF ROSLIN	⓫	BURGUNDY
❷	FLANDERS	⓬	PROVENCE
❸	NORMANDY	⓭	LOMBARDY AND TUSCANY
❹	BRITTANY	⓮	ENGLAND
❺	LA ROCHELLE	⓯	GALICIA
❻	ANJOU	⓰	PORTUGAL
❼	GUYENNE	⓱	ARAGON
❽	LANGUEDOC	⓲	HOLY ROMAN EMPIRE
❾	CHAMPAGNE	⓳	MAJORCA
❿	BAR		

THE ARK OF THE COVENANT, WHICH WAS BUILT AT THE BEHEST OF MOSES DURING THE EXODUS FROM EGYPT. IT WAS ALLEGEDLY USED TO CARRY THE TABLETS OF STONE ON WHICH GOD HAD INSCRIBED THE TEN COMMANDMENTS.

SECRET MEETINGS

There is a belief that the idea of founding the Templars was conceived far earlier than the twelfth century. For example, it is a matter of record that members of twelve leading aristocratic Rex Deus families in Scotland met regularly at Roslin long before the First Crusade, and continued to do so for many centuries afterward. Similar meetings can be traced in France in the county of Champagne and also in southern Provence, that also considerably precede the generally accepted date of the foundation of the order. A similar secret meeting of knights was convened after the fall of Jerusalem, to offer the throne of the newly conquered territories to Godfroi de Bouillon, the Duke of Lower Lorraine in France. Godfroi, the senior member of the Rex Deus at the time, claimed to be a direct descendant of Jesus. He refused the title of king, preferring to be known as the Protector of the Holy Sepulchre, which still carried all the royal responsibilities and prerogatives. The leading Rex Deus members had achieved their primary aim of returning the throne to one of its own; they now had to consolidate their position and use it to full advantage. They then called upon other members—including the Count of Champagne, André de Montbard, his nephew Bernard de Fontaines-les-Dijon, and Hughes de Payen—for further concerted action. The center of Rex Deus activity became the city of Troyes in the county of Champagne in eastern France. Members of Rex Deus from the families of Brienne, de Joinville, Chaumont, and Anjou met in Troyes with the Count of Champagne in 1104 and, after that meeting, Count Hughes I of Champagne left for the Holy Land and did not return until 1108.

THE FOUNDATION OF THE KNIGHTS TEMPLAR

Archbishop Guillaume de Tyre, writing several decades after the events, places the foundation of the Knights Templar in 1118. However, the Bishop of Chartres had made reference to "la milice du Christ" (the knighthood of Christ) in 1114, suggesting that the Templars may have been formed prior to 1118. Count Hughes I of Champagne traveled to the Holy

A DEPICTION OF CRUSADERS LEAVING TROYES IN THE COUNTY
OF CHAMPAGNE AT THE BEGINNING OF THE FIRST CRUSADE.

THE ORIGINAL KNIGHTS TEMPLAR

THERE WERE NINE FOUNDING MEMBERS OF THE ORDER OF THE KNIGHTS TEMPLAR, ONE OF WHOM REMAINS UNIDENTIFIED: HUGHES DE PAYEN ✣ GODFROI DE ST. OMER PAYAN DE MONTDIDIER ✣ ANDRE DE MONTBARD ARCHAMBAUD DE ST. AMAND ✣ GEOFFROI BISOL ROSSAL ✣ GONDEMAR ✣ UNNAMED

Land in 1114, accompanied by Hughes de Payen, one of the cofounders of the order. This trip earned the count a rebuke from the Bishop of Chartres for abandoning his wife and vowing himself to the "knighthood of Christ," in order to take up "that gospel knighthood by which two thousand may fight securely against him who rushes to attack us with two hundred thousand." Writing in 1135–37, a monk of St. Bertin in northwest France stated that the first Templars were knights who decided to stay in the Holy Land after the First Crusade. There are other enigmatic references to the order prior to the generally accepted date of its inception, suggesting that there was a long-standing hidden agenda underpinning the creation of the Knights Templar.

AN EARLIER FOUNDATION DATE?

At Roquebillière, a village in the southeast of Provence near the present city of Nice, there is evidence of a visit made to the village by a group of knights on their way to the principality of Seborga in northern Italy. After a brief stay at the village the group made their way through the Col de Turini to Seborga, where an archive of documents has recently been discovered. Nearby are the ruins of a Cistercian monastery that was originally founded by Bernard of Clairvaux in 1113, allegedly to protect some, unspecified, "great secret."

Under the direction of the abbot, Edouard, the monastery housed two knights who had joined the Order of the Cistercians at the same time as both Edouard and Bernard of Clairvaux. On becoming monks the two knights had taken the names Gondamar and Rossal. One document claims that Bernard came to the monastery at Seborga in 1117 with seven companions, released the two monks from their vows, and blessed the group prior to their departure for Jerusalem, an event that was delayed until November 1118 for reasons that aren't specified. Gondamar and Rossal's companions are listed as André de Montbard (Bernard of Clairvaux's uncle), Count Hughes I of Champagne, Payen de Montdidier, Geoffroi de St. Omer, Achambaud de St. Amand, and Geoffroi Bissol—all of whom (with the exception of Hughes of Champagne) are listed as the founders of the Knights Templar.

The document also records that Hughes de Payen was named as the first Grand Master of the Poor Militia of Christ by Bernard, a position in which he was consecrated by Edouard of Seborga. This account reinforces the tradition that links Hughes of Champagne with the alleged conspiracy that led to the foundation of the Order of the Knights Templar. All of the participants in the order's foundation were linked by a complex web of family relationships. Hughes de Payen was part of a cadet branch of the family of Champagne, and a vassal of the count, who was also his cousin, as was Bernard of Clairvaux. All of the other founding knights were related either by blood or by marriage to the Count of Champagne.

There is a later tradition that suggests that the Cistercians and the Templars were not merely associated with each other, but were linked so closely that some authorities claim that they were two arms of the same body. In 1202, the Master of the Order, Philip de Plessis, wrote to the abbot of

Citeaux asking for their prayers, adding, "And since our House took its institution from yours and your predecessors, it seems to us that we are especially bound to love you and you similarly ought to love us."

ARRIVAL IN JERUSALEM

The new order of knights was supposedly created to protect the pilgrimage routes in the Holy Land. On their arrival in Jerusalem the knights presented themselves to King Baldwin II, the younger brother of Godfroi de Bouillon. They informed him that they intended to found an order of warrior monks so that "as far as their strength permitted, they should keep the roads and highways safe … with special regard for the protection of pilgrims." They also swore to hold all their property in common.

The knights were given quarters in the palace that the king had made out of the al-Aqsa mosque on the southern edge of the Temple Mount, an area known to the crusaders as the Temple of Solomon and, in 1120, they received recognition from the patriarch of Jerusalem, Daimbert, the archbishop of Pisa, yet another cousin of Bernard of Clairvaux and the senior Catholic churchman in Jerusalem.

For the first nine years of their existence the Knights Templar wore ordinary clothes, the same as secular knights, but in their ninth year they were permitted to wear a white cloak or mantle, white being the symbol of purity. The patriarch gave them their first insignia, a red two-barred cross that later became known as the Cross of Lorraine, which was used as a symbol of the Free French forces during the Second World War. It wasn't until Eugenius III became pope that they embellished their mantles with the red *croix pattée* (an equal-armed cross with an expanded end), a symbol indicating that they were Christ's knights, and an emblem of martyrdom.

LEFT: THIS STONE CARVING AT THE VILLAGE OF ROQUEBILLIERE IN PROVENCE, SIGNIFIES A VISIT BY THE KNIGHTS TEMPLAR WHO STAYED HERE BEFORE JOURNEYING TO SEBORGA IN NORTHERN ITALY.

RIGHT: A LATE-MEDIEVAL DEPICTION OF PILGRIMS APPROACHING ONE OF THE GATES OF THE HOLY CITY OF JERUSALEM.

In 1120, Fulk of Anjou, the Count of Anjou and Maine, who later became king of Jerusalem between 1131 and 1143, made a pilgrimage to the Holy Land and joined the order as an associate. He was so impressed by Hughes de Payen that on his return to France he endowed the order with a regular income, 30 pounds of Anjou, the silver coinage of the region. A number of other French nobles followed his example. In 1125, Count Hughes I of Champagne returned to Jerusalem, having repudiated his wife and disinherited his son. He left the county of Champagne in the hands of his nephew and took the vows of chastity, poverty, and obedience as a Templar.

BERNARD OF CLAIRVAUX

The enigma of the foundation of the Knights Templar is compounded by the mysterious involvement of Bernard of Clairvaux. In 1112, this young Burgundian nobleman, Bernard de Fontaines-les-Dijon, had been admitted to the Cistercian Order, an offshoot of the Benedictines, which had been founded to reinstate the spiritual and temporal austerity of the original Benedictine rule. The order was struggling and in danger of collapse when Bernard announced his intention to join it. At first, his family were horrified and opposed his plans, but soon changed their minds. Not only did Bernard enter the monastic life, but 35 of his close male relatives and friends accompanied him, including

his elder brother Guy (who was heir to the estates and married with children), his two younger brothers, and his uncle, Gaudri of Touillon. This sudden influx of new members more than doubled the struggling order's numbers. Three years after their admission, Bernard and 12 other monks, including two of André de Montbard's brothers, started a monastery on land given by Count Hughes of Champagne, which they called Clairvaux. Bernard was appointed to the position of abbot of the new Cistercian Abbey of Clairvaux when he was only 24 years of age. It is perhaps not surprising to discover that most of these new recruits owed feudal allegiance to the Count of Champagne.

The Cistercians lived very simple and austere lives, trying to cut themselves off from the outside world. Their austere lifestyle and white habits—which were made from white, undyed wool—were mirrored by the new order of the Knights Templar, whose support by Bernard is extensively documented. The abbey buildings were also very plain and austere, as were those of the Templars. The Templar rule stated that, like the Cistercians, they would not admit women or children. These and other parallels indicate a close relationship between the two orders, suggesting that Bernard carried a great deal of influence in the formation of the Order of the Templars.

DIFFERENT TEMPLAR NAMES

THE ORDER OF THE KNIGHTS TEMPLAR WAS KNOWN BY A VARIETY OF NAMES: THE POOR FELLOW-SOLDIERS OF JESUS CHRIST AND THE TEMPLE OF SOLOMON, THE KNIGHTS OF THE TEMPLE OF SOLOMON, THE KNIGHTS OF THE HOLY GRAIL, THE KNIGHTS OF THE TEMPLE, THE TEMPLE, OR SIMPLY THE TEMPLARS.

ABOVE: THE TWO-BARRED ORTHODOX CROSS (4) GIVEN BY THE PATRIARCH OF JERUSALEM TO THE KNIGHTS TEMPLAR FOR USE AS THEIR INSIGNIA. THE SAME CROSS LATER BECAME MORE WIDELY KNOWN AS THE CROSS OF LORRAINE. THREE VARIANTS OF THE CROIX PATTÉE (1, 2, 3), THE INSIGNIA MOST COMMONLY ASSOCIATED WITH THE KNIGHTS TEMPLAR AND DISPLAYED ON THEIR TUNICS, CLOAKS, AND SHIELDS. A CROIX PATTÉE HAS ARMS THAT NARROW TOWARD THE CENTER.

RIGHT: BERNARD OF CLAIRVAUX ROSE TO A POSITION OF INFLUENCE IN THE CHURCH AND WAS AN EARLY SUPPORTER OF THE TEMPLARS.

BERNARD OF CLAIRVAUX'S RISE TO POWER

Bernard of Clairvaux, as he now became known, rose rapidly within the Church to a position of extraordinary power, and, although he was never to lead the Cistercian Order, his influence throughout Europe was immense. In the religious sector, he became personal adviser to the pope. Indeed, two popes, Honorius II and Eugenius III, had been pupils of his. In the secular world, his advice was sought by kings, emperors, and the nobility. However, his power did not stem solely from his influential connections. He inhabited a world where many preached the Christian virtues but few practiced them. Bernard constantly chastised the rich and powerful for their lapses and, as a result of this attitude, he became the living embodiment of the conscience of Christendom. His intellect was renowned and he demonstrated this in his sermons on grace, free will, and the Old Testament. Bernard was deeply committed to initiatory spirituality and preached 120 sermons based on the *Song of Songs* by King Solomon.

THE COUNCIL OF TROYES

King Baldwin had written to Bernard from Jerusalem, at Hughes de Payen's request, asking for his help in drawing up a Rule of Life, a system of regulations laying out the rights, obligations, and duties of all members of given religious orders. He was also asked to obtain papal approval of the order. Two knights were sent to Bernard with this request: André (who may have been Bernard's uncle, André de Montbard) and Gondamar. As a result, the Council of Troyes was convened on January 14, 1129, chaired by the papal ambassador, the Cardinal Legate of France, Matthew of Albano. At the time Bernard was stricken with a fever but, despite his ill health, he obeyed an imperative summons to attend the Church council where he dominated the proceedings. The minutes were kept by a Jean Michel, who said that he did so "by order of the council and of the venerable Father Bernard, abbot of Clairvaux," whose words were "praised liberally" by the assembled prelates.

On January 31, Hughes de Payen, accompanied by Godfroi de St. Omer, Achambaud de St. Amand, Geoffroi Bisot, and Payen de Montdidier, appeared before the council where they were presented with their rule by Bernard of Clairvaux. Bernard announced that the mission to Jerusalem had been fulfilled. Fearing that the authorities in the Vatican would sequester the finds made by the Templars, he stated that, "The work has been accomplished with our help, and the Knights have been sent on a journey through France and Burgundy, where all precautions can be taken against all interference by public or ecclesiastical authority." It is obvious from this statement that some of the artifacts discovered by the Templars in their excavations were sent to Burgundy for safekeeping. The Duke of Burgundy was a member of the Rex Deus families and yet another relative of André de Montbard, one of the founders of the Templar Order.

THE COUNTS OF CHAMPAGNE

The counts of Champagne ruled an area to the east and southeast of Paris measuring more than 7,969 square miles (20,640 square kilometers). They were leading members of Rex Deus and were virtually independent, owing nominal allegiance to the kings of France, the Holy Roman Emperor, and the Duke of Burgundy. They were linked by blood and marriage to the Capetian kings of France, the Norman and Plantagenet kings of England, and the St. Clairs of Normandy and Roslin. Count Hughes was openly involved in gnostic spirituality, a pathway of initiation and knowledge leading to enlightenment, and had given his support and protection to Solomon ben Isaac, the distinguished Jewish scholar. More well-known as Raschi, Solomon ben Isaac had founded an influential and internationally renowned Cabbalistic school of Judaic studies at Troyes in 1070.

Nine years after the foundation of the Knights Templar Bernard wrote a discourse on the order, "In Praise of the New Knighthood." This was addressed to Hughes de Payen, the first Grand Master of the Order and one of its cofounders. The last paragraph reads, "Hail, land of promise, which, formerly flowing with milk and honey for thy possessors, now stretchest forth the food of life, and the means of salvation to the entire world." Some translations give the last phrase as "from which will come the salvation of the entire world."

OMNE DATUM OPTIMUM

THE PAPAL BULL OF 1139 THAT ESTABLISHED THE NEW ORDER AS AN EXTREMIST ORDER OF THE CHURCH, ANSWERABLE ONLY TO THE PAPACY.

The Order may keep the booty it captures from the Muslims.

✣

Donations to the Order are confirmed.

✣

The Order's Rule of life under the Master is confirmed.

✣

The Brothers may elect their Master without interference from anyone else.

✣

The customs and observances of the Order cannot be infringed or changed except by the Master and with the consent of the wiser part of the Chapter of Brothers.

✣

The Brothers should not give oaths of loyalty or homage or any oaths to anyone outside the Order.

✣

No professed Brother may leave the Order to return to the secular world or join another religious Order.

✣

They need not pay tithes on the produce of their own lands.

✣

They may receive the right to collect tithes as a gift from laypeople or clergy, with the consent of the bishop or clergy concerned.

✣

They can remove these priests if they disturb the peace of the Order or the house or are useless, with the consent of the wiser part of the Chapter.

✣

The Order can have its clergy ordained by any bishop.

They may receive respectable clerks and priests who are ordained according to canon law (as far as they can tell) to serve the Order. They have to get the consent of the priests' bishops to do this. But if the bishop refuses, the pope will overrule him.

✣

Those priests who stay a year and are approved of by the Brothers may take the profession of the Order, swearing to obey the Master, and remain in the Order. They will have the same support and clothes as the Brothers except for their priestly vestments. They are only responsible for "care of souls" as far as the Order requests. They are not to be subject to anyone outside the Order (for example, the bishop).

✣

These clergy are not to preach for money, unless the Master makes arrangements for this.

✣

The pope lays down the procedure for the admittance of priests to the Order.

✣

The Brothers may build oratories wherever they live, and they can hear divine office there, and those who die as Brothers of the Order can be buried there.

✣

Wherever the Brothers go, they may have their confessions heard by any Catholic priests, or receive unction or any sacrament.

✣

These papal privileges and protection are extended to cover their household and servants.

the growth of the order

THE ORDER EXPANDED RAPIDLY, ACCEPTING DONATIONS OF LAND, AND BECAME INVOLVED IN BUILDING, MINING, AND VINICULTURE, PROTECTING THE PILGRIM ROUTES, CREATING AN INTERNATIONAL BANKING SYSTEM, AND SAFELY TRANSPORTING FUNDS TO FINANCE THE CRUSADES IN THE HOLY LAND.

F ollowing the circulation in 1129 of Bernard of Clairvaux's tract, "In Praise of the New Knighthood," new recruits and gifts of land and money flowed rapidly to the new Order of the Knights Templar. The tract extolled the virtues of the order and outlined the immense spiritual benefits that would accrue to those who supported its aims with acts of personal service and donations of land or money. The initial gifts of land, in Scotland, England, Champagne, and Provence, had long been planned for and were followed by donations of estates, castles, towns, farms, and villages throughout Christian Europe. A European network of Templar holdings was soon created, with many of them strategically placed near the most important trade and pilgrimage routes.

ACQUISITION OF LAND

In the years immediately following the Council of Troyes, grants of land, castles, and other properties came so rapidly that the order had to postpone garrisoning some of them for several years, owing to a shortage of manpower. When Hughes de Payen returned to the Holy Land in 1129, accompanied by 300 knights drawn from the noblest families in Europe who had rushed to become members of the order, he left a number of his lieutenants in Western Europe. Their mission was to raise recruits and solicit donations of property and money. Payen de Montdidier, one of the founding knights, was put in charge of recruiting in the area north of the River Loire in France, where he received donations of land as well as money. Others discharged a similar duty in the areas of Carcassonne and Provence, and a future Master of the Order, Robert de Craon, took donations in Barcelona. Monetary gifts could range from one denier (the smallest coin) to the rent of a small parcel of land, or more substantial gifts such as the rights to run mills or hold markets.

THE TEMPLARS' INFLUENCE THROUGHOUT EUROPE AND PARTICULARLY IN FRANCE, ITALY, AND ENGLAND WAS ALWAYS CLOSELY ALLIED TO THE CISTERCIAN RELIGIOUS ORDER.

In England the most extensive gifts of land were in Yorkshire and Lincolnshire, where, like the Cistercian monks, the Templars bred sheep and exported wool to the weavers of Flanders. The order not only made a significant contribution to the agricultural economy of these two English counties, they also recruited new members from the families who had donated the land. Only the larger holdings were managed by the Templars; the smaller ones were sublet. Members of the aristocracy made generous donations of land and money to the rapidly growing order, among whose ranks were soon numbered representatives from all the leading families in Western Europe.

TEMPLAR HOLDINGS

The major centers of power and influence in the West were in France (which at that time, was only the Isle de France, the area immediately surrounding Paris), Provence, Champagne, Bar, England, Tuscany, and the area known today as the Languedoc-Roussillon. These centers were closely followed by Aragon, Galicia, Portugal, Scotland, Normandy, and the Holy Roman Empire. The Knights Templar also established important bases throughout the Holy Land as a result of their rapid growth in resources and skilled manpower, to the extent that they became one of the most significant forces within the kingdom of Jerusalem. Templar estates, of varying size, were scattered throughout Europe from Poland, Denmark, Scotland, and the Orkneys in the north, to France, Italy, and Spain in the south, and from the Atlantic coastline to the Holy Land. However, the most important of their 9,000 estates in Europe were in France.

Existing place names still evoke their Templar history. For example, in England there is Temple in Cornwall, Templecombe in Somerset, and the Temple in London (the center of the legal profession); in Wales there are Templeton and Temple Bar in the county of Dyfed. Scotland abounds with Templar names, such as Temple (previously Ballantrodoch) in Midlothian, Temple in Strathclyde, Templehall in Fife, and Templand in Dumfries and Galloway. In France, where the Templars held the most estates, names commemorating the order are also common: Doncourt aux Templiers, Templehof et Colmar, Bure-les-Templiers,

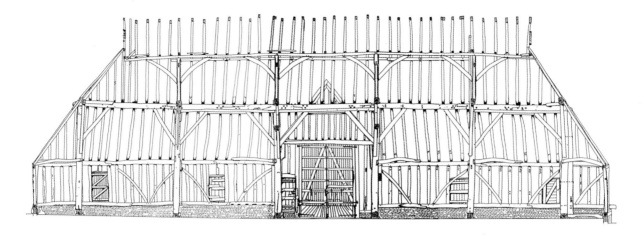

LEFT AND ABOVE: A TYPICAL THIRTEENTH-CENTURY BARN OF TEMPLAR CONSTRUCTION AT TEMPLE CRESSING IN ESSEX, ENGLAND, ONE OF AMONG 5,000 TEMPLAR SITES IN ENGLAND. THE DRAWING REVEALS THE SKELETON OF THE BARN'S TIMBER CONSTRUCTION.

RIGHT: A TEMPLAR ESTATE IN LEICESTERSHIRE, ENGLAND. ALL PROFITS FROM TEMPLAR HOLDINGS WERE SENT TO THE HOLY LAND TO MAINTAIN THE TEMPLAR FORCES.

Moissy-le-Temple, and Ivry-le-Temple. Spain, Germany, and other European countries also have their quota of names with Templar origins.

The Knights Templar were not the only beneficiaries of these generous gifts of land, for the previously struggling Cistercian Order also underwent an extraordinary period of rapid expansion; in the lifetime of Bernard of Clairvaux they established 300 new abbeys. At that time, the Orders of the Cistercians and the Knights Templar were looked on as two arms of the same body—the first a contemplative, monastic one, and the second, a strong, swift military arm of the same organization.

TEMPLAR ESTATES

The Templars owned land in every climatic zone in Europe. Although most of their holdings were not major fortified buildings, in Spain and Portugal castles were a necessity in the fight against the Moors. Some castles the Templars constructed were on defensive sites that posed major

difficulties for the builders; indeed they became renowned for strategically siting castles on the coast and rivers and building them with water gates.

On their own estates they built and maintained fortified farmhouses, barns to store corn, stables for their horses, dormitory blocks, workshops, chapels, and commanderies—administration centers that were often combined with lightly fortified agricultural buildings, prisons, or harbors. The nature of their holdings varied enormously, and included vineyards, pastures for sheep and cattle, mines, quarries, mills, smithies, and stud farms. In the main cities they erected strongholds that served to hold troops en route to the Holy Land and acted as secure places to keep treasure in transit. The Templar knights were warriors who needed servants, farriers for their horses, and armorers. Their farms required general laborers, blacksmiths, carpenters, and herdsmen, while their ships needed crews, carpenters, sail-makers, oarsmen, senior officers, and navigators. Their churches and chapels had their own chaplains, and they needed stonemasons.

TEMPLAR BUILDING

The Templars were involved in building projects from the time of their inception. The quarters they were given in the al-Aqsa mosque were adapted to their own use, and they were given free rein by the king to develop the area as they wished. In the 1170s, Theodorich, a German monk on pilgrimage, described how there were "houses, dwellings, and outbuildings for every kind of purpose," and how there were "lawns, council chambers ... and water in splendid cisterns." Theodorich went on to describe how the Templars had founded a new church "of magnificence and workmanship."

Examples of their particular architectural skills can be found in the fortresses in the East that they had constructed, rebuilt, or reinforced. The castle of Safed in Galilee, which controlled the road between Damascus and Acre and which they rebuilt in 1240, is one example of such a medieval masterpiece. In wartime it housed over 2,000 people, both civilian and military.

Templar masons were involved in the building boom that took place in the Holy Land from about 1130 onward. Among their major architectural projects were the construction of a new Church of the Holy Sepulchre in Jerusalem—which was dedicated in 1149; the renovation of the Church of the Nativity in Bethlehem; and the provision of an elaborately decorated tomb for King Baldwin IV on his death in 1185.

TEMPLAR CASTLES

In 1149, the order was given the fortress of Gaza. The knights guarded it and used it as a base from which to mount raids against the Muslims and to protect the southern frontier of the kingdom against Egypt. In 1152, the Bishop of Tortosa handed responsibility for the town's castle over to the Templars, exempting their chapels from his authority and reducing the tithes they had to pay. The Templars built a new castle for the protection of the townspeople and the bishop.

Castles in the East had a variety of functions. They provided a safe haven for the members of the order and their tenants when Muslim raiders swept across the countryside, as well as offering a place of refuge for allies of the order and anyone else fleeing from the Muslims. In the late 1170s, Saladin's great-nephew was captured by a renegade Christian knight who took him to the Templar castle at Safed where he was held prisoner until Saladin paid a heavy ransom for him. Saladin's forces swept over the land in 1180, bringing a complaint from the contemporary historian, Guillaume de Tyre, that the Knights Templar and the Knights Hospitaller had not sallied forth to engage him in battle but had remained in their castles. Rather than attack against overwhelming odds the knights had obviously considered that, in this instance at least, discretion was the better part of valor.

From the 1250s, the secular nobility gave or sold many castles to the Templars because they could no longer afford to garrison or maintain them, bringing additional power and influence to the already powerful order. However, this largesse also stretched their resources to the limit.

In addition to renovating old castles the Templars constructed many new ones. Between 1217 and 1221, the Templars built a new fortress on a headland to replace their watchtower at 'Atlit on the coast road between Haifa and Caesarea. They named it Castle Pilgrim in honor of the pilgrims who helped with the construction. Stones from a previous wall built by the Phoenicians were used, and in the process a hoard of ancient coins was discovered which was put to good use, helping to defray the costs of the construction. From the middle of the twelfth century, many castles were built to a concentric plan, making it easier to counter the danger from the Muslims' siege machinery. However, there have been suggestions that this style of building meant that the central enclosure housed the brothers and their chapel, while the mercenaries and other lay people inhabited the outer enclosure, thereby separating the religious order of knights from the secular inhabitants.

TEMPLAR CHURCHES

The classic round Templar church, with its distinctive features founded on octagonal geometry, was supposedly based on the design of the Church of the Holy Sepulchre in Jerusalem. The round churches formed only a small part of the Templar church-construction program, and are comparatively rare. However, those that were built have a Cabbalistic significance that has yet to be explained. Most Templar churches, especially those in southern Europe, are rectangular and have apsidal ends—a curved end to an otherwise rectangular building. The apse is always in the east. They are generally small and undecorated, apart from occasional decoration around the capitals of pillars and sometimes in the form of frescoes on the walls.

The attribution of churches to the Templar Order usually depends on archival sources that clearly state their Templar ownership, such as deeds showing the source of their donation or bills of purchase, or a recorded exemption from

FAR LEFT: CASTLE PILGRIM, ON THE COAST BETWEEN HAIFA AND CAESAREA, WAS NAMED AFTER THE PILGRIMS WHO HELPED BUILD IT. LIKE MANY TEMPLAR COASTAL CASTLES IT COULD BE APPROACHED FROM THE SEA BY A WATER GATE.

BELOW: AL KARAK IN JORDAN. CONSTRUCTION BEGAN ON THE CASTLE IN THE 1140S. ITS POSITION EAST OF THE JORDAN RIVER ENABLED THE CONTROL OF ROUTES FROM DAMASCUS TO EGYPT AND MECCA.

taxes, or on the method of their construction. Owing to their plain nature, few Templar churches have been identified as such on the grounds of their decorative style. However, the French Templar scholar, J.-A. Durbec, has listed six signs that have become the accepted standard of judgment where the origin of a particular church is in dispute (see the panel, right). All of the symbols shown are part of standard Christian iconography, but when three or more are found in any building constructed between 1127 (the date of the Templars' return to Europe after their foundation) and 1307 (the date on which the Templars were arrested in France) we can be almost certain of the accurate attribution of the building to the Templars.

In Provence and the Languedoc, lands once subjected to Templar rule, the Templar churches are dedicated almost without exception to Mary Magdalene and John the Baptist, both figures who would have been of supreme importance to the inner circle of the Order. John the Baptist is now accepted by many as the man who initiated Jesus into the

KEY TEMPLAR SIGNS	
	CARVINGS OF A FIVE-POINTED STAR ("L'ETOILE")
	CARVINGS OF THE TEMPLAR SEAL OF TWO BROTHERS ON ONE HORSE ("DEUX FRERES SUR UN SEUL CHEVAL")
	A REPRESENTATION OF THE TEMPLAR SEAL KNOWN AS THE AGNUS DEI ("UN AGNEAU PASCAL, NIMBE OU NON, TENANT UNE CROIX PATTEE AU DESSUS DE LUI")
	A STYLIZED REPRESENTATION OF THE HEAD OF CHRIST IMPRINTED ON A CLOTH SUCH AS THAT ON THE SHROUD OF TURIN OR THE VEIL OF VERONICA (THE MANDYLION)
	A DOVE IN FLIGHT CARRYING AN OLIVE BRANCH IN ITS BEAK ("UNE COLOMBE TENANT EN SON BEC UNE BRANCHE D'OLIVIER")
	A FORM OF ORIENTAL DECORATED CROSS (THE FLORIATED CROSS)

ABOVE: THE TEMPLAR CHURCH AT ST. TYRSE NEAR TRIGANCE, PROVENCE. AT DAWN ON THE FEAST DAY OF JOHN THE BAPTIST (JUNE 24) A BEAM OF LIGHT ILLUMINATES THE ALTAR.

spiritual mysteries, and Mary Magdalene as an important disciple of Jesus. One church at Trigance, in Provence, is constructed in such a way that at dawn on the feast day of John the Baptist a beam of light illuminates the altar with a golden glow. In most of these churches carvings of the crucifixion are noticeable by their absence but carvings of John the Baptist abound. A substantial number of them also house, or have housed, a statue of the Black Madonna. A carving or painting of a madonna and child whose features are deliberately depicted as black, the Black Madonna is believed by many to be symbolic of Mary Magdalene with the son she bore Jesus.

The majority of surviving Templar churches are to be found in France. However, one outstanding example is that of Temple Church in London, the Templars' English headquarters, a lasting memorial to the order.

GOTHIC CATHEDRALS

On a larger scale the Templars were involved in the financing and construction of many of the early Gothic cathedrals. The English architectural historian Fred Gettings states that the Order of the Knights Templar was closely involved in the era of cathedral construction known as the Rise of the Gothic, and that they not only gave moral support to the building of cathedrals throughout Europe but that they were also often involved in financing them. The flowering of the Gothic style of architecture brought a new era of church design that enabled cathedrals to be built far higher than ever before, with more windows and the creation of larger naves and greater spaces within them. This architectural form first arose after the Templars returned from Jerusalem but, strangely, there is no developmental period from the Romanesque style that had preceded it. Did the Templars find the key to this new style of building among the documents they discovered under the Temple Mount? Or did they learn it in the Holy Land from the Saracens? Gordon Strachan, who has made an in-depth study of Gothic architecture, believes that the pointed arch which provides the foundation of this style of building came from the Holy Land. He claims that it resulted from "a unique blending of indigenous building skills with the architectural genius of Islam" and that the Templars first became aware of the method of designing the pointed arch from their contact with the Sufis of Islam. During their first nine years in Jerusalem, the Templars met many Sufis and gained knowledge of this form of sacred geometry from them. They first used it in the Holy Land, for in Jerusalem, on Temple Mount, the Templars built a three-bayed doorway with pointed arches.

The architecture of the Gothic cathedrals is phenomenal, and it is claimed that Gothic architecture—the fruit of Templar knowledge of sacred geometry—was not just an example of architectural beauty but a three-dimensional

ABOVE: THE GOTHIC STYLE OF ARCHITECTURE HERALDED A NEW ERA OF CHURCH DESIGN AND ENABLED CATHEDRALS TO BE BUILT FAR HIGHER THAN PREVIOUSLY.

code that passed a hidden message in an architectural form of *la langue verte*—the green language, or language of initiation (a verbal code used to speak without fear of being reported to the church authorities).

The cathedrals of Chartres and Amiens in France were heavily influenced by Templar principles of sacred geometry and were possibly also used as vehicles to encode heretical messages within the symbolism of church art. Yet according to the Church the cathedral at Chartres, a legacy to the Templars' direct involvement and beliefs, was built from the cooperative efforts of the townspeople and the pilgrim trade, which financed this magnificent building.

CHARTRES CATHEDRAL

Chartres Cathedral in France was erected in the almost unbelievable time of 26 years. Massive and immediately accessible financial resources were required to complete this vast and complex edifice in such a short time. It is highly unlikely that the proceeds from the pilgrims who visited Chartres during its construction would have paid for even the stained glass in the windows, much less for the construction and decoration of the whole building. The only credible source of finance available in Europe at that time for the undertaking of such a project was the Order of the Knights Templar.

Chartres Cathedral has been described as "a hymn to gnostic, initiatory spirituality; a melodic symphony in stone that is a visible celebration of divine harmony." On a column in the north porch, known as the Portal of the Initiates, can be found a carving of the Ark of the Covenant being transported on a wheeled wagon, possibly alluding to the legend that Hughes de Payen brought the Ark to Chartres where it was concealed in the crypt, until at a later date it was, allegedly, transported to Scotland to the safekeeping of the St. Clairs of Roslin.

AMIENS CATHEDRAL

The present cathedral at Amiens was built on the site of its predecessor (destroyed by fire in 1218) and is said to celebrate the gnostic principle of divine wisdom, or Sophia, and to house the reliquary containing the head of John the Baptist. This strange artifact was brought to Amiens from Constantinople by Walter de Sarton in 1206, and has remained in the cathedral ever since. Evidence of the importance of this relic to the cathedral is shown in the transept on a series of carved panels that depict the biblical story of John the Baptist, and in superbly sculpted scenes in bas-relief that decorate the outer wall of the choir. These show in vivid detail episodes from the life and death not of Jesus the Messiah and supposed Son of God, but of John the Baptist, the man who many claim initiated Jesus into the spiritual mysteries. One scene shows the severed head of John the Baptist on a platter, being pierced in the temple with a knife. This practice was apparently repeated in Templar and Masonic burials for many centuries but its significance is unknown. Evidence of this can be seen at a small Templar church in Bargemon in Provence, where a crypt was discovered containing a row of skulls and long bones; each skull had been pierced in exactly the manner as shown on the carving at Amiens.

THE MEDIEVAL CRAFTMASONS

The great Gothic cathedrals were mainly the work of a guild of specialist masons known as the Children of Solomon, who left their mark in the form of the *chrisme à l'epée*—a Celtic cross enclosed within a circle. The Children of Solomon, who were named after King Solomon, the

LEFT: THE WEST FRONT OF AMIENS CATHEDRAL WAS BUILT AFTER A FIRE IN 1218 DESTROYED THE ORIGINAL BUILDING. IT WAS FINANCED BY THE TEMPLARS IN ORDER TO HOUSE THE RELIQUARY CONTAINING THE HEAD OF JOHN THE BAPTIST. THE HEAD HAD RECENTLY BEEN BROUGHT BACK FROM CONSTANTINOPLE.

RIGHT: KING LOUIS VI OF FRANCE WATCHING MEDIEVAL STONEMASONS AT WORK.

legendary builder of the temple where the Knights Templar had their first quarters, were taught the principles of sacred geometry by the Cistercians. Apprentices learned their trade from skilled masons or companions as they moved from site to site throughout the country in what was known as a "tour de France." When they had attained the necessary levels of skill and qualification they were initiated by their masters into conclaves known as *cayennes*. Their initiation involved moving through three separate degrees in order to qualify as a master mason; first they were initiated as an apprentice, then they went on to the degree of companion, and finally when they were considered to have honed their skills sufficiently they then attained the degree of master. Many of the Templar churches in Provence and the Languedoc were built by a group of craftmasons, Companonnage Tuscana, who were an offshoot of an Italian order that claimed connection with Numa Pompelius, a legendary Roman king.

THE COMPANNONAGE

THE CRAFTMASONS OF THE COMPANONNAGE WERE DIVIDED INTO THREE GROUPS:

✣ THE CHILDREN OF SOLOMON WHO WERE RESPONSIBLE FOR BUILDING THE GREAT GOTHIC CATHEDRALS.

✣ THE CHILDREN OF MASTER JACQUES (WHO WERE ALSO KNOWN AS LES COMPAGNONS PASSANT), ONE OF WHOSE PRIMARY FUNCTIONS WAS BRIDGE BUILDING.

✣ THE CHILDREN OF FATHER SOUBISE, RESPONSIBLE FOR CONSTRUCTING ECCLESIASTICAL BUILDINGS IN THE ROMANESQUE STYLE, CHARACTERIZED BY ROUNDED ARCHES, MASSIVE VAULTING, AND THICK WALLS.

A mysterious relationship existed between the Knights Templar and the Children of Solomon that is still far from clear. It has not been possible to discover whether the Children of Solomon were an integral part of the Templar Order, simply affiliated with it, or just employed by the knights. However, it is indisputable that the Templars gave a Rule of Life to the Children of Solomon in 1145 on the instructions of Bernard of Clairvaux. The Rule was given by a superior authority and, just as Bernard was the superior authority who gave the Templars their Rule, the Templar Order, as the principal employer and patron, gave the Children of Solomon their Rule. This was prefaced by the words, "We the Knights of Christ and of the Temple follow the destiny that prepares us to die for Christ. We have the wish to give this rule of living, of work, and of honor to the constructors of churches so that Christianity can spread throughout the earth and not so that our name should be remembered, Oh Lord, but that Your Name should live."

The theory that these masons had an intimate connection to the Templar Order seems validated by the fact that they were granted considerable privileges by both the Church and the state. These included freedom from paying taxes and immunity from prosecution by the builders of secular buildings, yet when the Templars were suppressed the Children of Solomon lost all their privileges and immunities at the same time.

THE TEMPLAR FLEET

As a result of their twofold interest in protecting pilgrims and maintaining communications with their bases in the Holy Land, the Templars operated a well-organized fleet that exceeded that of any state. They owned a large number of ships that plied the Mediterranean between bases in Italy, France, Spain, and the Holy Land. The fleet included a number of highly maneuverable, small, fast war galleys fitted with rams, and cargo ships for carrying troops, horses, commercial cargoes, and passengers—pilgrims en route to or from the Holy Land. Special ships were used for transporting horses: the smaller ones were capable of carrying on average 40 horses (as well as 40 foot soldiers, all their arms, and 30 oarsmen to man the ship) and the larger vessels of carrying a hundred horses. The transporters were often built with stern doors that allowed mounted knights to embark directly onto the beach.

In the first half of the twelfth century, the Templars had to rely mainly on the ships of others, but by the thirteenth century the order possessed its own ships. Having their own fleet gave the Templars independence in the Mediterranean and enabled them to provide a steady stream of military traffic. Their main base was situated on the island of Majorca. On the Atlantic coast of France their principal port was the highly fortified harbor of La Rochelle, where they were exempted from paying harbor dues by Eleanor of Aquitaine. In Toulon at the beginning of the thirteenth century, the feudal lords granted the Templars the right to build houses and fortifications wherever they wished, making a safe harbor for their ships, which were permitted to load, unload, and transport horses tax-free.

The Templars traded with the British Isles from La Rochelle and it is alleged that they also traded with Greenland, the North American mainland and Mexico, probably by "island hopping" along the old Viking route, but there is, as yet, no evidence to support this. Did La Rochelle hold some special significance for the Templars? It is too far

THE TEMPLARS OWNED A VAST FLEET OF VESSELS FOR SHIPPING BOTH MEN AND HORSES TO AND FROM THE HOLY LAND.

north to make a viable embarkation point for the Holy Land, for which they had other ports further east, such as Marseilles. This suggests that the allegations of voyages and trade to the west may have some degree of plausibility.

Owning their own fleet brought benefits that spread far beyond the Templar Order. It allowed the Templars to act as a reliable channel of communication between the East and the West. Important letters, often from the king of Jerusalem to people in Europe, including the pope, were entrusted to the knights for safe delivery. Indeed, their reputation for integrity and reliability made them the perfect couriers for diplomatic and commercial matters. Furthermore, their protection of the trade and pilgrimage routes ensured growing prosperity for the merchant classes, for guarding the highways ensured every traveler's safety. Thus people from all walks of life right across Europe benefited greatly from the order's activities and power.

Their fearsome reputation as fighting men and defenders of Christianity allied to their ownership of large estates in every corner of Europe and their financial shrewdness and reliability led to them being given positions of responsibility in almost every kingdom in which they operated.

the templars in the east

THE KNIGHTS TEMPLAR, THE PRIMARY CRUSADING MILITARY ORDER IN THE EAST DURING THE TWELFTH AND THIRTEENTH CENTURIES, FOUGHT ALONGSIDE BOTH THE KNIGHTS HOSPITALLER AND SECULAR KNIGHTS IN THE CAMPAIGNS AGAINST THE MUSLIMS, AND OFTEN ACTED AS ADVISERS TO THE LEADERS OF THE CRUSADES.

The Order of the Knights Templar portrayed itself as the most important defender of Christendom—a view shared by many others. Outwardly it was a religious military order that was no different from the Knights Hospitaller or, later, the Teutonic Knights. The ordinary brothers were orthodox Christians and therefore dedicated to defending Christendom against the Muslims and retrieving and retaining control of the holy places in Palestine. The leading knights, as members of Rex Deus, fought fanatically for the Holy Land, which they regarded as rightfully theirs. Some of the order's activities in the kingdom of Jerusalem drew much criticism, but, despite this, it was seen as the major military force in the East and held more responsibility for the defense of the Holy Land than any other order. It has been estimated that the Templars had a standing army of 300 knights in the crusader states and the kingdom of Cyprus, as well as several thousand men at arms and many squadrons of turcopoles, or mercenary cavalry. Houses of brothers were maintained in the major towns, villages, and fortresses, many of which had been donated to the order, others bought or constructed by the knights themselves.

The Knights Templars played a major role in all of the Christian army's expeditions in the Holy Land, acting as rearguards or vanguards while the army was on the march. During the Second Crusade they protected the rear of the army on its march through Asia Minor. On the march from Acre to Jaffa in 1191, during the Third Crusade, the Templars helped to maintain discipline among the Christian forces. However, as far as the travelers to the Holy Land were concerned, the Templars' most important role was their protection. The Templar castles guarded the pilgrimage routes, and the knights acted as military escorts to the pilgrims when they visited the holy places.

There were many Italian communes in the crusader states, made up of merchants from Genoa, Pisa, and Venice, who carried almost as much influence as the military orders.

TEMPLAR KNIGHTS FIGHTING THE SARACENS AT THE
BATTLE OF ASCALON, WHICH WAS FINALLY TAKEN
ONLY AFTER A SIEGE LASTING MANY MONTHS.

Some lived permanently or most of the time in the East, others came each year in the spring and fall to buy and sell their merchandise. The merchants carried on the trade that brought considerable wealth to the crusader states. They also transported pilgrims, colonists, and supplies from Europe. Their ships provided a form of sea power that gave them a definite advantage over the Muslims. In ports such as Acre and Tyre they had their own quarters and were granted various privileges, including the right to hold their own courts and deal with their own legal matters.

THE KNIGHTS HOSPITALLER

The Order of the Knights of the Hospital of St. John, or Knights Hospitaller, had preceded the Knights Templar, having been formed as a hospital in the mid-eleventh century in Jerusalem by Italian merchants from Amalfi in order to cater for the needs of sick pilgrims. Soon after the foundation of the Templars, the Hospitallers began to expand their operations from merely caring for the sick to becoming a military order in their own right. Despite this dramatic change of purpose, the Grand Master of the Knights Hospitaller was nonetheless compelled to serve as an orderly in the hospital as part of his sacred duty until the end of the order's existence.

The first references to the Hospital of St. John in Jerusalem date from about 1065. Like the Knights Templar, the details surrounding the foundation of the Knights Hospitaller are obscure and the original founder has never

THE KNIGHTS HOSPITALLER

THE ORDER OF THE HOSPITAL OF ST. JOHN OF JERUSALEM, OR THE KNIGHTS HOSPITALLER, WAS FOUNDED IN THE ELEVENTH CENTURY AS A MONASTIC BROTHERHOOD PROVIDING MEDICAL SERVICES TO PILGRIMS AND CRUSADERS IN THE EAST. AFTER THE FIRST CRUSADE IN 1099, THE ORDER BEGAN TO INCLUDE DEMOBILIZED KNIGHTS, WHO EVENTUALLY BECAME COMBATANTS AS WELL AS MEDICS, FIGHTING ALONGSIDE THE TEMPLARS. THERE WAS DEEP ANTAGONISM BETWEEN THE TWO ORDERS THROUGHOUT THEIR CAMPAIGNS IN THE HOLY LAND WHICH CONTINUED AFTER THE FALL OF THE KINGDOM OF JERUSALEM WHEN THE HOSPITALLERS RELOCATED FIRST TO THE AEGEAN AND THEN TO MALTA.

been accurately identified. So a mythology was created that credited the order with far grander beginnings than were in fact the case. This legend claimed that the order had existed since the time of Jesus' apostles, or even from the time of the Maccabees, a Jewish dynasty of patriots, high priests, and kings who, 200 years before Jesus, rebelled against their Greek overlords. Jesus himself was said to have visited the hospital on many occasions, performing miracles while there; and the Virgin Mary supposedly lived in the hospital for three years before ascending to Heaven.

In 1113, the Hospitaller Order was granted papal protection and privileges in a bull issued by Pope Paschal II, *Pie Postulatio Voluntatis*, which gave papal protection and privileges to the Hospitallers and allowed brothers and professed members to elect their own Grand Master without reference to any other authority. It also confirmed the title to the great number of possessions that had already been

given to the order. After the success of the First Crusade the Order of the Knights Hospitaller received many donations, both from the crusaders who remained in the Holy Land and from donors in Europe who wished to support the work of the hospital and share in the spiritual benefits that accrued. With these large donations the order was able to become a strong, viable, and truly independent institution, whose sole purpose at that time was caring for the sick.

By the time of Pope Paschal's bull the Hospital of St. John had already begun to gain financial independence from the ecclesiastical hierarchy in the kingdom of Jerusalem. In 1112 it had been exempted from paying tithes, and Pope Paschal's privilege meant the Hospital could keep the tithes from land that the order itself cultivated. This income could then be used to provide medicine and provisions in its role as carers for the poor and the sick. Pope Innocent II's bull of 1137 permitted the Hospitallers to build villages, churches,

and cemeteries on deserted land they had been given, for the use of the general populace. They were permitted to build private chapels elsewhere, but for their own use only. The nature of the order began to change to a warrior status, and they were now allowed to have priests and clerics within its ranks, provided that these had been ordained. These clerics were answerable only to the pope—they were exempted from the authority of the diocesan bishop. Without the permission of the brothers or Master of the Order, no member was allowed to leave. Like the Knights Templar and the Cistercians, later privileges placed the order under the authority of the pope alone. By 1154, a succession of papal privileges had freed the order from the jurisdiction of the patriarch of Jerusalem and all the bishops and archbishops throughout Christendom, ensuring that the order was able to continue its work unhindered by local regulations and taxes, a situation that led to numerous disputes with the clergy.

THE TEUTONIC KNIGHTS

A latecomer to the military orders in the East were the Teutonic Knights, established in 1190 after the Third Crusade. German crusaders had arrived in the Holy Land in 1197, but most of the knights returned to their homeland after they had failed to make much military contribution, their sole success being their participation in the capture of Beirut. A few knights remained, however, and they were welcomed into the fold of a field hospital that had been set up in 1190 by German merchants. The hospital had first operated in 1191 at the siege of Acre, where its base had been set up in a tent made from a ship's mainsail. Brothers from the Hospital of St. Mary of the Germans, founded in 1127, joined the new hospital. When the knights were added to the contingent they became the Teutonic Knights of St. Mary's Hospital and were formally recognized as an order by the Church on March 5, 1198. The Teutonic Knights were the last of the three great military orders. The new order adopted the Templar Rule. Its knights wore a white mantle like the Templar habit but emblazoned with a black cross. These facts have led some authorities to claim that the Teutonic Knights were an offshoot of the Templars, an idea that has never been proven.

FAR LEFT: RUINS OF PART OF THE HOSPITAL OF ST. JOHN IN JERUSALEM, WHICH WAS CONSTRUCTED c.1056 AND USED TO HOUSE AND TREAT THE SICK AMONG THE MANY THOUSANDS OF PILGRIMS VISITING THE HOLY CITY.

ABOVE: AN EIGHTEENTH-CENTURY PRINT OF A CONTEMPORANEOUS KNIGHT OF THE ORDER OF ST. JOHN OF JERUSALEM, ALSO KNOWN AS THE KNIGHTS HOSPITALLER OR THE KNIGHTS OF MALTA.

THE TEUTONIC KNIGHTS

THE TEUTONIC KNIGHTS WERE FOUNDED IN THE 1190-91 AS A HOSPITAL ORDER TO CARE FOR SICK AND WOUNDED GERMANS. AFTER 1211, THEY SHIFTED THEIR ATTENTION AWAY FROM PALESTINE TO FOCUS ON THE NEW CRUSADES IN THE BALTIC STATES. OVER THE NEXT 50 YEARS, THEY SUBDUED PRUSSIA AND MANY OF THE EAST BALTIC STATES, RETAINING A FIRM HOLD OVER THE BALTIC AND NORTHERN GERMANY. THE POWERFUL REGIME THEY ESTABLISHED FLOURISHED FOR 300 YEARS AND ONLY WENT INTO DECLINE IN THE FIFTEENTH CENTURY.

THE FIRST TEMPLAR FORTRESS

In the 1130s, the Templars were given responsibility for patrolling the frontier region between the kingdom of Cilicia, now southern Turkey, and the principality of Antioch. Their first major fortress was consequently not in the kingdom of Jerusalem but in the north of the crusader states in the Amanus Mountains, a narrow range running south from Asia Minor which creates a natural barrier.

The Templars' task was to guard the Belen Pass, or the Syrian Gates, through these mountains. The stronghold of Barghas was strategically situated on an impenetrable summit on the eastern side of the range and gave the knights a clear view over the Plain of Aleppo below. This and other passes in these mountains were secured not only against the Muslims but also against the Cilician Armenians and Byzantine Greeks.

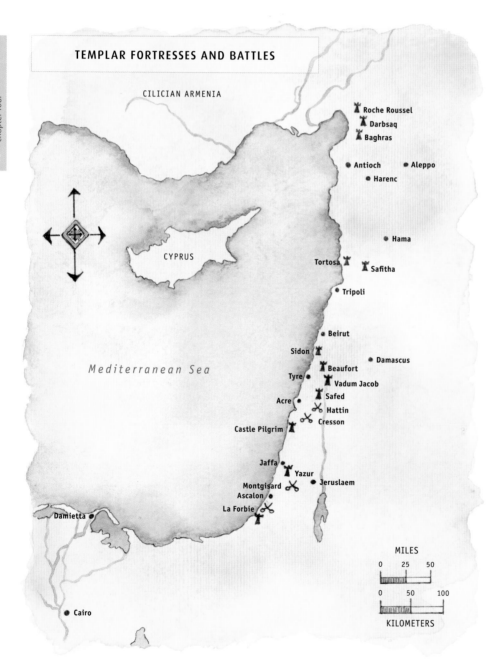

TEMPLAR FORTRESSES AND BATTLES

CILICIAN ARMENIA

♰ Roche Roussel
♰ Darbsaq
♰ Baghras

● Antioch   ● Aleppo
● Harenc

CYPRUS

● Hama

Tortosa ♰
♰ Safitha

● Tripoli

Mediterranean Sea

● Beirut

Sidon ♰
● Damascus
♰ Beaufort
Tyre ●
♰ Vadum Jacob
Acre ●
♰ Safed
⚔ Hattin
⚔ Cresson

Castle Pilgrim ♰

Jaffa ●
♰ Yazur
Montgisard ⚔ ● Jeruslaem
Ascalon ●
La Forbie ⚔

Damietta ●

MILES
0   25   50

0   50   100

KILOMETERS

● Cairo

RIGHT: A FRESCO OF AN EARLY TEMPLAR KNIGHT WITH A COUCHED LANCE AND NORMAN ALMOND-SHAPED SHIELD OR *ESCARBOUCLE.* THE PAINTING ALSO SHOWS A FLEUR-DE-LIS, THE BLAZON OF THE ROYAL CAPETIAN HOUSE OF FRANCE.

LEFT: THE HOLY LAND DURING THE CRUSADER PERIOD ILLUSTRATING THE KEY TEMPLAR FORTRESSES AND THE LOCATIONS OF SIGNIFICANT BATTLES.

TEMPLAR RAIDS

The Templars and the Hospitallers were always viewed as a serious threat by the armies of Islam. The Templars were described by Saladin's secretary as "rebels, demons, evil men, with their castles built on inaccessible crags which were the lairs of wild beasts." Therefore Muslims felt that they had good cause to rejoice in every victory won over the military orders, and turned every such event into a celebration.

The Templars' actions against the Muslims were far from being purely defensive, for they believed in attack being the best form of defense. In consequence, as well as taking a full part in all military expeditions, they mounted many raids against their foes. Many were for the capture of animals, people, and booty that could be utilized to good advantage or converted into wealth. The fortress of Gaza was specifically constructed for the Templars to launch raids on the city of Ascalon and to attack the caravans sent by the caliph of Egypt with supplies for the city.

Raids were risky, however, and many had disastrous results. One led by the Templar Grand Master Robert de Craon against an invading Turkish force in 1139, near Hebron, resulted in many of the knights being killed. In another raid in 1237, the Templars set out from Barghas, rode into an ambush, and were all slaughtered.

MILITARY ADVISORS

The Templar Order played an important part in military expeditions and acted as military advisers on many occasions. In this manner, members of Rex Deus were placed in positions of immense power and influence. Everard des Barres, who was the Grand Master of the Temple at the time of the Second Crusade, was one of King Louis VII's most trusted advisers. Indeed, during the Third Crusade the

Templars had to advise King Richard I of England that an advance on Jerusalem was doomed to failure as it would be impossible to hold the city if it was captured. On other occasions their pragmatic advice led to them being labeled cowards, particularly when they suggested a truce with the enemy. In February 1250, at Mansurah, during the First Crusade of King Louis IX of France, both the Templars and Hospitallers advised against a cavalry charge. They were overruled by the king's younger brother, Count Robert of Artois, who accused them of cowardice. The charge went ahead and almost everyone was killed, including the count. The whole affair was a disaster, but the advice given by the military orders had been vindicated.

A FEARSOME ARMY

The Templars and Hospitallers were highly trained professional soldiers, and the Templars' reputation was unsurpassed. Their rule demanded that they fight for the benefit of Christendom, and Rex Deus tradition dictated that the families worked and fought for the benefit of the community in which they lived and not for their own glory. They were excellent at mounted warfare, and, at this time, the cavalry charge was the most effective military maneuver. The Templars used cavalry, made up of mounted knights and sergeants, as well as employing infantry, archers, and men-at-arms carrying axes and spears. However, the cavalry charge was the main form of attack, and the cavalry operated according to a strict set of rules. The opening move in most engagements came from the archers, who fired at the enemy to split their lines, and provide cover for the charge. When the archers ran out of ammunition, the cavalry charged, punching through the enemy lines. In the wake of the cavalry came the foot soldiers, who dispatched any of the enemy unseated by the

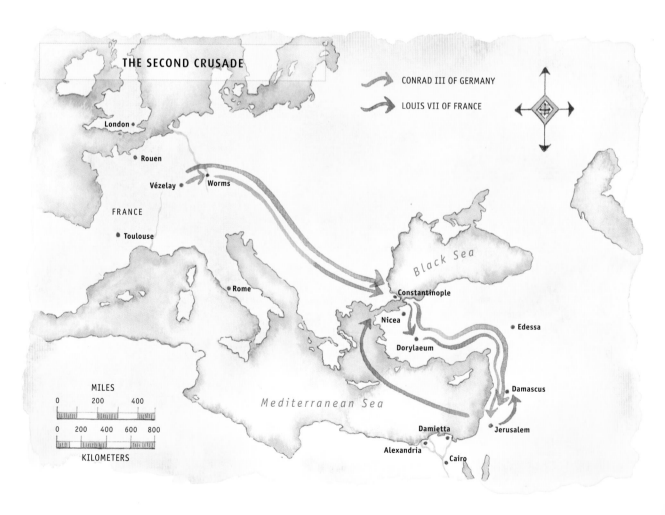

mounted knights. Being mounted on horseback gave the knight the advantage of height and speed, and was the preferred method of fighting. Even the horses were trained to kick, butt, and bite. Templar knights, who were all nobly born, had attained knighthood prior to joining the order. Thus they had undergone prolonged training and learned many more skills than were needed for fighting in the infantry. Secular knights had a heavy financial investment in the form of weapons and horses; the order provided the equipment for its own knights.

At the Battle of Arsuf in 1191, the rearguard commanded by the Hospitallers was described as riding "so close together that an apple thrown into their midst would not fall to the ground without touching people or horses." A well-timed charge by such a closely knit, heavily armored group had a devastating effect on enemy lines, with their soldiers being mown down as the cavalry charged. The Templars had the reputation of always being the first to enter the fray and the last to leave it. They swore never to leave the field of battle as long as their standard, the beauseant, was still held aloft. The beauseant was carried by the gonfanier (banner-bearer) and represented the order's presence on the battlefield. It was also the focal point to which the knights would withdraw and regroup before mounting another charge. If the beauseant did fall, any remaining Templars would rally first to the standard of the Knights Hospitaller, or, if that too had fallen, to any other Christian banner. The Templars had a fearsome reputation as the best-trained soldiers in the East and were renowned for their almost suicidal bravery in their earlier years. However, by the beginning of the thirteenth century they had learned to be more cautious in battle.

LEFT: THE SEPARATE ROUTES OF THE FRENCH AND GERMAN FORCES. THE GERMANS MET WITH STRONG RESILIENCE IN CONSTANTINOPLE AND WERE ONLY ABLE TO ADVANCE WHEN THE FRENCH ARMY ARRIVED.

ABOVE RIGHT: A CRUSADER KNIGHT KNEELING IN PRAYER BEFORE GOING INTO BATTLE. THE TEMPLARS WERE PARTICULARLY RENOWNED AS SKILLED AND FEARSOME WARRIORS.

THE SECOND CRUSADE

By the time of the Second Crusade (1147–49) the Templars were well-established in the Holy Land. News of the fall of the city of Edessa in 1144 reached Pope Eugenius III in the fall of 1145, whereupon he wrote immediately to King Louis VII of France, begging him to lead a new crusade and retrieve Edessa from the Saracens. Three years earlier, Louis had illegally seized land from his most powerful vassal, Theobald of Champagne, and this had precipitated a civil war. The king's barons showed a marked lack of enthusiasm for an expedition to the East, and even his own chief adviser, Abbot Suger of St. Denis, advised against it. An agreement was reached between Louis and his barons that the matter would be settled at Vézelay in Burgundy on March 31, 1146. Louis turned to the greatest orator of the twelfth century, Bernard of Clairvaux, for help in raising a crusading army. The crowd who gathered to hear Bernard preach the crusade was too large to fit in the small church at Vézelay, so Bernard delivered his sermon from a specially constructed platform, built at the edge of the town. At the end of Bernard's speech, King Louis was first to take the Cross, followed by many members of the nobility, including his brother Robert, the Count of Dreux. Bernard continued his recruitment drive in the north of France and Flanders. Unable to cross the Channel to proselytize in person, because of his poor health that made it difficult for him to travel, Bernard wrote letters to potential crusaders in England, stressing their good fortune at being given the chance to save their souls.

On April 27, 1147, King Louis and Pope Eugenius were welcomed at a chapter meeting at the Templar headquarters in Paris, along with four archbishops, 130 Templar knights (many recalled from Portugal and Spain), and an equal number of Templar sergeants and squires. The pope imposed a tax on all Church goods to raise finance for the crusade, and appointed the Templar treasurer to receive the proceeds.

THE FIRST DEFEATS

The Second Crusade was a disaster from start to finish. King Conrad III of Germany had joined the crusade, and he set out for the Holy Land ahead of the French, traveling across Anatolia, but suffered an early defeat at the hands of the Seljuk Turks. The French king, however, sent the Grand Master of the Templars, Everard des Barres, to Constantinople to negotiate with the Byzantine emperor for a passage through his territory. Permission was granted—albeit grudgingly, for there was still considerable distrust between the Eastern and Western Christians.

In January 1148, demoralized at the news of the German contingent's defeat, the French army came under persistent attack in the Cadmus Mountains, where their heavy cavalry were at a grave disadvantage. The crusaders, by now acutely short of food, water, and ammunition, were being subjected to continuous attacks by the Turkish light cavalry, whose archers were adept at firing from the saddle. The French army was in danger of falling apart, when Louis turned to the Templar Master, Everard des Barres, for advice. The army was divided into units of 50, each with a Templar at its head, which gave the beleaguered French crusaders a much-needed morale boost, enabling them to reach the port of Attalia, from where Louis took his best troops to Antioch by boat, leaving the remainder to find their own way. The chronicler who wrote an account of the journey made by Louis VII to Jerusalem during the crusade, Odo of Deuil, praised the Templars' discipline and the aid they gave the army as it traveled through Asia Minor.

MONEY RUNS SHORT

The expense of getting the army across Asia Minor had left Louis almost destitute, and he turned to the Templars for help. On May 10, the Grand Master sailed to Acre, where he managed to raise sufficient funds for the king's needs from the Templar treasury and by using the order's possessions as security to raise loans. The king was now in debt to the Templars for the sum of 2,000 silver marks, a sum equal to half the income from his royal estates in France. Once more the vast resources of the Knights Templar and their financial acumen had come to the aid of a cash-strapped European monarch. This was not to be the last time a crusading French king was to be bailed out by the Templar Order.

At a council of war at Acre in June it was decided that the army would make for Damascus, with the attack planned for July. The siege began successfully from the west, but the crusaders made an ill-advised decision to move to the east of the city, a position that had no easy access to water and

CROWDS GATHER TO HEAR THE GREAT MEDIEVAL CHURCHMAN, BERNARD OF CLAIRVAUX,

PREACHING THE SECOND CRUSADE AT VÉZELAY IN BURGUNDY, AT THE BEHEST OF POPE EUGENIUS III.

faced the most heavily fortified area of the walls. However, it was a position from which they could deploy their heavy cavalry. When rumors of an advancing Muslim army reached the Christians, they lost their nerve and retreated, signaling the ignominious end of the crusade.

GAZA AND THE SIEGE OF ASCALON

In 1149, King Baldwin III of Jerusalem gave the city of Gaza to the Templar Order. It was the first important fortress that the order received in the kingdom of Jerusalem, and although the city was largely in ruins the Templars soon set about rebuilding the castle. Previously, King Fulk had built a number of fortresses to encircle the city of Ascalon, which not only protected the coastal road leading to Egypt but also provided a base for Muslim raids on Christian settlements. Gaza was the final fortress in the encirclement of the city and effectively ensured that Ascalon was now completely cut off. The Egyptian forces unsuccessfully attempted to retake Gaza almost as soon as the Templars had acquired it.

The Christians laid siege to the heavily fortified city of Ascalon on January 25, 1153. The siege lasted until August, when the crusaders' mobile siege tower was set alight by a

sortie of defenders from the city. Unfortunately for them, the wind changed direction and blew the flames against the city walls, causing the masonry to crack and part of the wall to collapse. A unit of 40 Templars rushed forward under the leadership of the Grand Master, Bernard de Tremelay. According to Guillaume de Tyre, the Templar greed for booty was so great that the Grand Master forbade any non-Templars from entering the city, which gave rise to future accusations of avarice. The Templars made a stand in the city but were annihilated and the following day their headless bodies were displayed on the city walls. The city fell a week later, however. The Egyptian occupants were allowed to leave with their portable belongings. They were forced to leave behind large quantities of treasure and arms. André de Montbard, the uncle of Bernard of Clairvaux and one of the founding knights, succeeded Bernard de Tremelay as Grand Master but he held the post for only three years. He was succeeded in 1156 by Bertrand de Blanchfort.

CAMPAIGNING IN EGYPT

The rest of the 1150s and 1160s saw no major battles, merely raids by one side against the other, with the Templars taking a prominent role on the Christian side. Things began to change in 1162, when King Baldwin III died and was succeeded by his brother, Almaric, who had his sights set on Egypt. In the fall of 1163, he launched a campaign against

THE SIEGE OF DAMASCUS IN 1148 BEGAN SUCCESSFULLY BUT, FEARING ATTACK FROM THE MUSLIM ARMY, THE CRUSADERS RETREATED, SIGNALING AN IGNOBLE END TO THE SECOND CRUSADE.

RAYMOND OF TRIPOLI

WHILE A PRISONER OF THE MUSLIMS, COUNT RAYMOND OF TRIPOLI LEARNED TO SPEAK ARABIC, STUDIED THEIR CULTURE, AND LEARNED SOMETHING OF THEIR PSYCHOLOGY. HE WAS SUPPORTED BY THE KNIGHTS HOSPITALLER AND BY FAMILIES THAT WERE LONG ESTABLISHED IN JERUSALEM BUT WAS OPPOSED BY THE KNIGHTS TEMPLAR AND THE MORE RECENTLY ARRIVED SETTLERS. LED BY REGINALD OF CHATILLON, THEY WANTED TO ACQUIRE LAND AND WERE IMPATIENT FOR WAR. THEY ACCUSED THE COUNT OF BEING IN ALLIANCE WITH SALADIN.

Cairo in which the Templars took part under the leadership of Bertrand de Blanchfort. The crusading army was forced to retreat when the Egyptians breached the dykes in the Nile delta. Undaunted, Almaric returned in 1164, but ultimately came to an agreement with the Egyptians that both the Christian and Muslim armies would withdraw.

During Almaric's absence from the kingdom of Jerusalem, Antioch was attacked by a large Muslim force. Against the advice of most of his advisers, including the Templars, Prince Bohemond III of Antioch ordered an attack against this much larger force; his army was routed, and all but seven of the 60 Templar knights were killed. Two years later, Christian forces, with many Templars among them, were besieged in a cave-fortress in Transjordan. Almaric and his troops raced to the rescue but, before they reached the fortress, they were met by 12 Templars, who informed the king that the fort had surrendered to the Muslims without a fight. This angered Almaric to such an extent that he ordered the execution of the Templars and they were all hanged. Two years later, in the fall of 1168, he launched a full-scale invasion of Egypt in which the Templars, not surprisingly, refused to take any part whatsoever.

Almaric died in 1174, having dissipated the strength of the kingdom of Jerusalem with his repeated forays into Egypt. He was succeeded by his 13-year-old son, Baldwin IV, who was a leper. As Baldwin was too young to rule, his cousin Count Raymond III of Tripoli elected to act as regent. It was at this time that the crusaders' greatest adversary emerged, Salah ad-Din Yusuf ibn-Alyub, better known as Saladin.

the beginning of the end

BY THE END OF THE TWELFTH CENTURY, THE CRUSADERS BEGAN TO LOSE GROUND. THE LOSS OF THE CASTLE AT JACOB'S FORD, THE DEBACLES AT THE SPRINGS OF CRESSON AND HORNS OF HATTIN, COUPLED WITH THE FALL OF JERUSALEM SIGNALED THE DECLINE IN POWER OF THE CHRISTIAN KINGDOM IN THE EAST.

In his youth Saladin had been drawn to a peaceful, religious life. However, he became convinced that only a jihad (holy war) would drive the invaders out of Palestine and, by using diplomacy and military prowess, he went on to unite the many squabbling and disparate factions within Islam. Highly respected by Muslims and Christians alike, Saladin had a well-earned reputation for courtesy and chivalry toward his enemies. He is reputed to have shown compassion for the Christian captives held in the dungeons of Damascus, giving them furs to keep out the icy cold. Unlike most of the members of the crusading armies, as a member of the Muslim elite, Saladin was literate and cultured. He was an expert swordsman and adept at using the lance. However, his courtesy and magnanimity did not extend to the military orders for whom he had an implacable hatred, although he did admire the fighting prowess of the secular knights in the crusading armies.

JERUSALEM UNDER THREAT

The Templars were soon engaged with Saladin's forces. In 1177, Saladin launched an attack on the well-defended fortress of Gaza, but at the last minute he changed direction and laid siege to Ascalon instead. Baldwin IV, who had now come of age, led the counterattack and reached the city ahead of Saladin. Realizing that Jerusalem was now undefended, Saladin made for the Holy City, leaving a small force to keep Baldwin occupied. Baldwin, however, realizing that he had been outflanked, summoned the Templars from Gaza, broke through Saladin's force at Ascalon, and raced after the Egyptian army, catching up with them at Montgisard. The Egyptian army was utterly defeated but Saladin escaped and returned to Egypt.

LEFT: THE MUSLIM SIEGE OF JERUSALEM BY AN ARMY OF NEARLY 2,000 MEN UNDER THE COMMAND OF SALADIN. THE CITY FELL IN 1187 AND ITS INHABITANTS WERE SPARED, IN CONTRAST TO THE MASSACRE THAT ENSUED WHEN THE CHRISTIANS TOOK THE CITY IN 1099.

ABOVE RIGHT: SALAH AD-DIN YUSUF IBN-AIYUB (c.1137–93), BETTER KNOWN AS SALADIN. HE UNIFIED THE DISPARATE FACTIONS WITHIN ISLAM AND WAS RENOWNED THROUGHOUT THE CHRISTIAN AND ISLAMIC WORLDS FOR HIS CHIVALROUS DEEDS AND HONORABLE BEHAVIOR.

JACOB'S FORD

Baldwin's force was not large enough to take advantage of the victory over the Muslims at Mongisard, and in the summer of 1179, Saladin laid siege to the chastellet ("little castle") at Jacob's Ford on the River Jordan. The attack took place before the castle's completion—only the first enclosure had been built. A peace treaty between Baldwin and Saladin, delineating the area as a nonmilitary zone, had forbidden either side from building castles on this frontier, but the Templars claimed that they were not bound by the agreement. Baldwin had in effect broken the treaty by building the castle, albeit under pressure from the Templars, who decided that one was needed on this site to protect the road to Damascus.

Baldwin set out to relieve the castle on June 10. Saladin's force repelled the attack, and a number of knights were taken captive, among them the Grand Master of the Templars, Odo de St. Amand, who died in captivity the following year. Arnold of Torroja, an experienced mediator, succeeded Odo de St. Amand as Grand Master. He was aware of the internal disagreements between the Christian factions and, using his negotiating skills, brought them together to present a united front, knowing that their bickering could have fatally sapped their military strength. Saladin was also aware of the internecine strife between the Christians and patiently bided his time until he felt secure enough to attack.

Accompanied by the Grand Master of the Hospitallers and the newly elected patriarch of Jerusalem, Arnold of Torroja set off for Europe to raise awareness of the threat posed by Saladin. Unfortunately, Arnold died in Verona, leaving the others to continue with their mission.

GERARD DE RIDEFORT

As Arnold's successor the Templars chose Gerard de Ridefort, who had a reputation for impatience and recklessness. His election in early 1185 coincided with the death of Baldwin IV, who was succeeded by his seven-year-old nephew, Baldwin V, with Raymond of Tripoli acting as regent. Under Gerard's leadership, the Templar Order became closely involved with the issue of who should succeed to the throne of Jerusalem after the death of Baldwin V, whose reign lasted only a year. The task of selecting a new ruler for the kingdom of Jerusalem then fell to the pope, the Holy Roman Emperor, and the kings of England and France.

However, before this selection took place, a coup d'état in 1186, by Sybil, the sister of Baldwin IV, placed her on the throne with her husband Guy of Lusignan as king. The main conspirator in the coup was the Templar Grand Master Gerard de Ridefort. The Grand Master of the Hospitallers, Roger des Moulins, on the other hand, disapproved of the coup d'état and tried to prevent the coronation. A weak king, Guy was immensely unpopular and universally despised. He was seen as a usurper by the majority of his nominal vassals and his seizure of the throne exacerbated the disunity among the Christians in the Holy Land. Eventually, a fatal rift occurred between the king and his chief allies, with Gerard de Ridefort and Reginald de Chatillon on one side and Raymond of Tripoli on the other.

THE SPRINGS OF CRESSON

Gerard de Ridefort tried to persuade the king and Raymond of Tripoli to heal the rift between them, but this plan fell apart when Raymond allowed a Muslim scouting party into the area around Tiberias on condition that it was non-aggressive. Gerard, who received word of this while en route to Tiberias with a contingent of Templars and a force of Hospitallers under Roger des Moulins, was incensed. He immediately set out to attack the Muslims, catching up with them at the Springs of Cresson, near Nazareth, where they were watering their horses. The Christian forces numbered only 140 knights (of which 90 were Templars),

RIGHT: A DEPICTION OF THE BATTLE AT THE HORNS OF HATTIN (1187). DUE TO COMPLETELY INEPT STRATEGY AND POOR GENERALSHIP, THE CHRISTIAN FORCES WERE SURROUNDED AND MASSACRED ALMOST TO A MAN BY A VAST SARACEN ARMY LED BY SALADIN.

LEFT: THE BREACH IN THE WALL AT THE FORTIFICATION OF JACOB'S FORD, WHICH WAS ATTACKED BY SALADIN IN 1179. THE TEMPLARS LATER BUILT A CASTLE ON THIS SITE.

while Saladin's army numbered 7,000. Gerard was urged to retreat by the Master of the Hospitallers and the Marshall of the Templars, but he accused them both of cowardice and ordered the knights to attack in a suicidal cavalry charge. In the bloodbath that ensued, only three Templars (one of whom was Gerard de Ridefort) escaped with their lives.

As a result of this debacle, the king and Raymond of Tripoli did bury their differences, while Saladin's army marched inexorably toward Jerusalem, taking the city of

THE HORNS OF HATTIN

By the end of June, nearly all the men capable of fighting—in total 20,000 troops of which 12,000 were cavalry—had gathered, leaving the cities and fortresses virtually undefended. The army was ordered to attack at dawn and made a forced march toward Tiberias, constantly harassed by Muslim archers and suffering from intense thirst. The Templars, who were acting as the rearguard, made a request to the king to stop for the night. Count Raymond, leading the

Tiberias on the way. A council of war of all the Christian forces was held at Acre. Raymond argued that Saladin would have difficulty holding his large army together in the summer heat, and advised the king to remain where he was as the Christian army was heavily outnumbered. Gerard de Ridefort and Reginald de Chatillon persuaded the king otherwise, accusing Raymond of cowardice, and the king ordered the Christian army to march toward Tiberias. At camp that night, Raymond once more advised the king against marching on Saladin's army, but, despite his apparent agreement to withdraw, later that night Gerard de Ridefort bullied the weak and vacillating king into changing his mind and launching an attack, convincing him that it would be shameful to sacrifice Tiberias.

vanguard, made the prophetic statement, "Lord God, the war is over. We are dead men. The kingdom is finished."

The army set up camp on an arid plateau below the Horns of Hattin. Below them they could see Saladin's army. The well at the nearby village of Lubiya was dry and they carried no water. Any soldier who went looking for water was captured by the Muslims and killed. Finally, Saladin's forces set fire to the scrub on the hill; a breeze fanned the flames, which crept relentlessly toward the thirsty Christian army. Crippled by lack of water and heat, the Christian forces did not stand a chance; they attempted to break through the Muslim ranks but were defeated. The armored knights repeatedly repelled the Muslim onslaught but to no avail—they were too weak, and gradually they were

SALADIN

SALAH AD-DIN YUSUF IBN-AIYUB (C.1137–93) WAS A KURDISH GENERAL WHO BECAME SULTAN OF EGYPT. AS A VIZIER HE CONQUERED EGYPT IN 1169 AND FOUNDED HIS OWN DYNASTY IN 1175. HE CONQUERED SYRIA AND TOOK JERUSALEM IN 1187, WHICH PRECIPITATED THE THIRD CRUSADE. HE WAS RENOWNED THROUGHOUT THE CHRISTIAN AND THE ISLAMIC WORLDS FOR HIS CHIVALRY AND GENEROSITY TO THE POOR OF ALL FAITHS.

overcome. The defeat of the Christian army was caused by a combination of Saladin's meticulous planning and superb skill on one side, and Gerard de Ridefort's arrogance and strategic incompetence on the other.

King Guy was captured, and, with the courtesy for which he was famous, Saladin offered the king a glass of ice-cooled water. According to Muslim tradition, a man who is offered food or water is spared. The king drank his fill, then offered it to Reginald de Chatillon, who reached out to take it—but, before he could drink, the glass was taken from him. Reginald was hated by Saladin, who reached for his scimitar and beheaded him.

The same fate befell all the Templar and Hospitaller knights. Saladin described them as "impure races," and vowed to "purify the land of these two monstrous orders, whose practices are of no use, who will never renounce their hostility, and will render no service as slaves." Every one of his soldiers who captured a knight was rewarded with a bounty of 50 dinars. The knights were offered the choice of death or conversion to Islam; they chose death. The Sufi members of Saladin's entourage decapitated them and, in all, 230 Templar and Hospitaller knights were executed—with the exception of Gerard de Ridefort whose life was spared. The week after the catastrophe at Hattin, Acre fell to Saladin's forces, followed soon after by Ascalon and Gaza. At Gaza, the Templar garrison, bound by their vows of obedience, surrendered at the command of their Grand Master, Gerard de Ridefort. Saladin's victory at Hattin not only defeated the largest ever Christian army to be assembled in the Holy Land it also signaled the final decline of crusader power there.

THE FALL OF JERUSALEM

Saladin's destination was Jerusalem, and he besieged the Holy City in 1187. The mobilization of most of the Christian forces in the Holy Land had left Jerusalem woefully underdefended; there were only two knights left in the city, and the situation was so serious that 30 men from the bourgeoisie were quickly awarded knighthoods. The outcome of the siege was a foregone conclusion, but the Christians threatened to raze the Dome of the Rock to the ground, forcing Saladin to parley. Saladin agreed to ransom every man, woman, and child in the city, many of whom were refugees from the surrounding countryside. The sum of 100,000 dinars was set, but such a large amount could not be found. The ransom was renegotiated, and it was agreed that the rate would be ten dinars for a man, five for a woman, and one for a child. The freedom of 7,000 refugees was bought with 30,000 dinars raised from public funds. Saladin entered Jerusalem in triumph on October 2.

The Temple Mount was surrendered, and the Templar administrative force was forced to vacate its headquarters in the al-Aqsa mosque, never to return. The Muslims purified the mosque with rosewater and installed a pulpit that had been commissioned in anticipation of the victory. Saladin once more showed his generosity, allowing the Church of the Holy Sepulchre to remain in Christian hands. However, the Cross was removed from the Dome of the Rock and dragged around the city for two days, where it was trampled on and beaten with clubs by the jubilant Muslims.

The triumphal entry of Saladin into Jerusalem and the way in which he treated the occupants shows a courtesy and generosity in total contrast to that shown at the time of the First Crusade when the crusaders slaughtered the inhabitants without quarter—Christian, Jew, and Muslim alike—until the blood and gore were ankle deep.

SALADIN GAINS GROUND

Saladin's triumphs over the Christian forces seemed endless. The fortress of Kerak in southern Syria was besieged for more than a year and capitulated only because the inhabitants were starving. The Templar castle of Safed was bombarded for a month before it surrendered. Many other

castles were lost, although the coastal cities of Antioch, Tripoli, and Tyre remained in the hands of the Christians. The arrival of a fleet of Sicilian galleys reinforced the garrison at Antioch, and the situation at Tyre changed when a force of crusaders arrived under the command of the German prince, Conrad of Montferrat. On January 1, 1188, Conrad's ships defeated the Egyptian fleet, forcing Saladin to abandon the siege.

In June 1188, King Guy was released from captivity after swearing that he would leave the kingdom. However, the Church assured him that a vow made under duress to an infidel was invalid. Guy then marched on Tyre with an assembly of knights who had been ransomed or released. Conrad of Montferrat refused him entry, on the basis that Guy's defeat had lost him his crown. After waiting outside the walls for several months Guy realized that he had to either reestablish his control or leave the Holy Land.

In August 1189, showing a hitherto unseen determination, Guy marched south to Acre accompanied by a force of Templars led by Gerard de Ridefort. The city had fallen to Saladin's forces after the disaster at Hattin. Guy besieged the city by setting up a fortified encirclement around it—even though part of Saladin's army was still in the area—following an audacious plan that was probably the suggestion of Gerard de Ridefort. The Grand Master died fighting near Acre on October 4, 1189, salvaging some of his reputation. Acre was finally retaken on July 12, 1191, and the Templars continued to lead the campaign to protect the remaining Christian possessions against Saladin.

When news of the fall of Jerusalem and the other severe losses in the East reached Europe, Pope Urban III was so shocked that he died. His successor, Gregory VIII, reigned for just two months, but, before his death, he called upon the kings of Europe to put an end to their hostility against each other and devote themselves to driving the Saracens from the Holy Land. Unlike the First Crusade, which had been seen as a means of gaining absolution, the Third Crusade was promoted to vanquish evil and prove courage on the battlefield.

THE MASSIVE FORTRESS OF KRAK DE CHEVALIERS BUILT BY THE KNIGHTS HOSPITALLER ON THE FRONTIER OF THE COUNTY OF TRIPOLI ON LAND DONATED BY COUNT RAYMOND II OF TRIPOLI.

THE THIRD CRUSADE

The third son of King Henry II of England was one of the first to respond to the pope's appeal. King Richard I, the Lionheart, had established his reputation as a ruthless ruler and a brilliant strategist and general during incessant struggles with rebellious vassals in Aquitaine. He was joined by King Philip II Augustus of France, who initially protested at Richard's impetuous action, but changed his mind after hearing a sermon from the archbishop of Tyre. Henry II was forced to join them, but died before fulfilling his long-term

LEFT: KING RICHARD I, THE LIONHEART, OF ENGLAND–A SUPERB SOLDIER OF CONSUMMATE SKILL WHO NONETHELESS MUST UNDOUBTEDLY RANK AS ONE OF ENGLAND'S WORST KINGS. HIS ENTIRE MILITARY CAREER IN THE HOLY LAND WAS SPENT FIGHTING AGAINST SALADIN, WHO TREATED KING RICHARD WITH GREAT RESPECT AND ABSOLUTE CHIVALRY.

RIGHT: A MAP OF THE THIRD CRUSADE SHOWING THE OVERLAND ROUTE OF THE GERMAN HOLY ROMAN EMPEROR, FREDERICK BARBAROSSA, VIA CONSTANTINOPLE. RICHARD I TRAVELED VIA MESSINA, OFF THE SOUTHERN TIP OF ITALY, CAPTURING IT BEFORE SAILING ON AND SACKING CYPRUS. KING PHILIP II OF FRANCE TOOK A MORE DIRECT ROUTE.

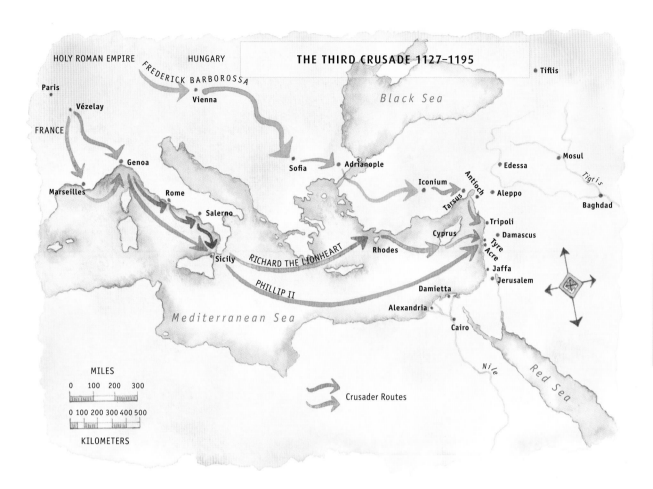

ambition to go on crusade. However, as king of England, Richard could now draw on the wealth of the country to finance his ambitious plans for the forthcoming crusade.

THE TAKING OF CYPRUS

King Richard's fleet set out from Marseilles, but the voyage was far from straightforward. One of his ships was wrecked on the coast of Cyprus, which was ruled by a renegade Byzantine prince, Isaac Ducas Comnenus, and the shipwrecked crusaders were thrown into the dungeons. When Richard arrived a week later he demanded their release, but Comnenus refused. Richard prepared for war and—supported by a fleet from Acre—he embarked on a lightning conquest of the island aided by the Knights Templar. After very little resistance Comnenus surrendered the island to King Richard, who left a small garrison in its fortresses and sailed on to Palestine. He landed near Tyre,

but King Philip and Conrad of Montferrat refused him entry so he sailed on to Acre, where his arrival gave a much needed morale boost to the crusaders.

THE SALE OF CYPRUS

Richard was given the leadership of the crusade, and his friend and vassal Robert de Sable was elected as Grand Master of the Templars. The Grand Master immediately bought the island of Cyprus from the English king for 100,000 besants. The Greek population on the island was uncontrollable, and Richard wanted nothing more to do with it. As soon as the agreement was reached, 20 knights with their squires and a number of sergeants were dispatched to take control. The knights were extremely unpopular, and on April 4, 1192, the garrison in Nicosia was besieged by the Greeks. The insurgents were dealt with but it was obvious that the island could not be controlled by a small garrison.

The Templars returned the island to King Richard, who immediately resold it to Guy of Lusignan, the former king of Jerusalem, for 60,000 besants, the balance of the original amount that was still owed by the Templars.

ACRE RECAPTURED

The main Templar force was heavily involved with the crusading army in the siege of Acre, which was retaken on July 12, 1191. The inhabitants were ransomed for 20,000 besants, and 1,500 Christian captives were released. Now that the city was again in Christian hands, many of the crusaders returned home. Saladin asked the Templars to guarantee the terms of an interim agreement concerning the exchange of prisoners and payment of the ransom, but they declined. Exasperated by Saladin's procrastination in keeping to the terms of the agreement, King Richard ordered the execution of 2,700 Muslim captives, among them women and children, which he personally oversaw.

As far as the Muslims were concerned, this was a clear breach of the treaty with Saladin. A different view was taken by the Christian chroniclers of the time, who believed that within the conventions of war Richard had acted out of necessity and was to be praised. After all, Saladin had ordered the massacre of the Knights Templar and Knights Hospitaller after his victory at Hattin.

The crusading forces now moved south toward Haifa and Caesarea, harassed by Saladin's forces. The Templars took the vanguard and the Hospitallers the rearguard, with the remaining cavalry riding in tight formation between them. Saladin mounted an all-out attack south of Caesarea but suffered his first real defeat in battle. After Christmas 1191, the Christian army marched to within 12 miles of the Holy City. The crusaders who had come from Europe with Richard urged him to lay siege, but the Templars advised caution on the grounds that even if they were able to take Jerusalem they would not be able to hold it when the crusaders left.

THE ARMIES OF RICHARD I OF ENGLAND AND PHILIP II OF FRANCE RE-TAKE ACRE ON JULY 12, 1191. SUBSEQUENTLY THE CITY BECAME THE TEMPLARS' HEADQUARTERS.

RICHARD I OF ENGLAND

RICHARD I, THE LIONHEART, WAS KING OF ENGLAND FROM 1189–99. THE THIRD SON OF HENRY II OF ENGLAND AND ELEANOR OF AQUITAINE, HE TOOK PART IN THE THIRD CRUSADE, LED BY PHILIP AUGUSTUS OF FRANCE, USING ENGLAND AS A SOURCE OF TAX REVENUE TO FUND HIS ACTIVITIES. HE WAS CAPTURED BY KING LEOPOLD V OF AUSTRIA IN 1192 AND RANSOMED IN 1194. BEFORE ACCEDING TO THE THRONE HE SPENT MOST OF HIS LIFE FIGHTING AGAINST HIS FATHER. HE DIED IN A MINOR SKIRMISH FIGHTING AGAINST HIS BROTHER JOHN IN FRANCE.

A PEACE TREATY

In 1192, Saladin led the attack on Jaffa and took the town after three days of heavy fighting. The garrison was on the point of surrender when King Richard arrived from Acre with 50 Pisan and Genoese galleys. Accompanied by 80 knights, 400 archers, and about 2,000 Italian marines, Richard soon had Saladin's army on the run. However, before more forces could reach Richard, Saladin counterattacked with skill and ingenuity. Richard's small force repeatedly fought off the Muslim attackers. When Richard's horse was killed, Saladin showed his courtesy and generosity yet again by sending Richard two fresh mounts as a gift.

This battle showed both leaders that neither could win outright, and that they would have to make a truce. Both had other matters that needed their attention. Richard agreed that Ascalon should be demolished. In return, Saladin guaranteed that the Christians would remain in possession of the coastal cities from Antioch to Jaffa, Muslim and Christian pilgrims would be free to cross each other's territory, and the latter were free to visit their sacred sites in the Holy Land. The peace was to be kept for the next five years with the aid of the Templars and the Hospitallers.

Richard returned to Acre and eventually set sail for Europe, having been away for 16 months. He was heavily criticized for his impetuosity in recklessly endangering his life, even though he was highly skilled in planning and logistics. One contemporary writer described him as one of the most outstanding warriors of European history.

the templar order in europe

THE TEMPLARS' PRINCIPAL PURPOSE IN EUROPE WAS TO GENERATE INCOME TO SUPPORT THEIR BROTHERS IN THE EAST. NONETHELESS, THEY PLAYED A PART IN THE RECONQUISTA, THE FIGHT TO RETAKE THE IBERIAN PENINSULA FROM THE MOORS, AND ALSO IN EASTERN EUROPE AGAINST THE MONGOL INVASION.

The activities of the Templar Order reached far beyond the Holy Land, for their original objective of protecting pilgrims was extended to the routes to the holy shrines of Europe, such as England's Canterbury Cathedral, Spain's Cathedral of St. James of Compostela (the most important site of all in the twelfth to fourteenth centuries), and Chartres, Mont St. Michel, and Rocamadour in France, as well as many others. A complex network of routes linked parts of Europe to Rome, Compostela, and every major population center.

However, the order's primary purpose remained the protection of the kingdom of Jerusalem. They earned vast sums from their extensive holdings in Europe (30 percent of which were in the Languedoc-Rousillon region of the south of France) and the profits from their banking activities. This constant stream of revenue was used to maintain the army in the Holy Land. By the early 1140s, the Templars had acquired enough land and recruits to enable them to maintain simultaneous military operations in both Palestine and the Iberian Peninsula. Indeed, it is probable that without this extensive support network the Order of the Knights Templar would have vanished from history with the first major defeat.

However, the Templars' activities in Europe were not all peaceful and commercial. From the early 1140s, the order played a major role in the Reconquista, the fight to retake Spain from the Moors that took place between the eleventh century and the end of the fifteenth century, and, to a lesser degree, they also played a part in the conflicts in Eastern Europe. The only crusade in which the military orders refused to participate was the Albigensian Crusade (1208–1244), which took place in the southwest of what is now France, in the area we know as the Languedoc-Rousillon. It was a crusade in which Christian fought against Christian.

KING ALFONSO OF ARAGON, WHO BEQUEATHED A THIRD OF HIS KINGDOM TO THE TEMPLAR ORDER. HE ACHIEVED SPECTACULAR VICTORIES AGAINST THE MOORS, CAPTURING SARAGOSSA IN 1118 AND LEADING A MILITARY RAID FAR INTO SOUTHERN ANDALUSIA IN 1125. HE WAS FATALLY WOUNDED IN BATTLE IN 1134.

MOORISH SPAIN

Moors from North Africa invaded Spain in 711, conquering most of the country with bewildering speed. Islamic rule in Spain spawned a highly sophisticated culture in which Christians and Jews were respected as "people of the Book" and treated with a degree of tolerance that was unimaginable in the rest of Europe. For the next 750 years, adherents of the three great monotheistic religions— Christianity, Islam, and Judaism—lived together in relative peace and harmony. Coexistence between the Christians and Muslims benefited them all, and some Christians even adopted Muslim customs without converting to Islam. Most Spanish Christians were proud to be part of the advanced culture that was found in Moorish Spain. The Muslims defeated in the Reconquista were, at first at least, allowed to keep their mosques open and continue to follow the religion of Islam, demonstrating the tolerance the different religious cultures extended toward each other in the Iberian Peninsula, in stark contrast to that shown to the Muslims by Christians elsewhere.

The Reconquista was recognized as a crusade, and in 1100 and 1101, Pope Paschal banned any Spanish knight from joining the crusade to the Holy Land while the Moors were still a danger, offering the same remission from sin as to those on the crusade to Jerusalem. At the beginning of the thirteenth century, a Christian army recruited from the different Iberian kingdoms defeated the Muslim forces and rapidly advanced southward until, by 1300, the Iberian Peninsula, except for Granada, was back in Christian hands for the first time in nearly six centuries.

THE IBERIAN PENINSULA

By the early 1130s, the Templars were building a close relationship with the rulers of Portugal and began to receive donations of land in that country; donations on the eastern side of Spain came more slowly. The order had been granted privileges in 1130 by King Alfonso of Aragon, the instigator of the Reconquista. The properties in the Iberian Peninsula were used purely as a source of income to support the knights in the Holy Land, and it was not until 1143, under pressure from King Alfonso's successor, that the Templars

reluctantly committed themselves to military action in the Reconquista, as a result of negotiations arising from the terms of King Alfonso's will.

In 1131, the childless King Alfonso bequeathed a third of his kingdom to the Templars, with the other two-thirds going to the Knights Hospitaller and the Church of the Holy Sepulchre in Jerusalem. When Alfonso died in 1134, his will was ignored but, ten years later, a settlement was reached in which the new king of Aragon granted the Templars a number of fortresses, exemption from various taxes, a fifth of all land captured from the Moors, a fifth of all the booty they captured, an income of 100 sous a year from Saragossa, and a tenth of all royal revenues. The new ruler also aided the Templars in building castles and fortresses to assist the campaign against the Moors. Henceforth the Templars became a major force in the fight against the Islamic invaders of Spain, acting in an advisory capacity and taking an active part in all the military campaigns. Although small in numbers, the Templars' strength lay in their ability to mobilize quickly and to remain in the field, unlike the secular nobles and their forces, who, once they had served their 40 days, returned to their homes and farms. As a standing army, the Templars were able to exert a far

A MEDIEVAL ILLUSTRATION SHOWING A KNEELING KNIGHT IN CHAIN MAIL COVERED WITH A SURCOAT ADORNED WITH THE TEMPLAR CROSS. IMAGES SUCH AS THESE WERE USED BY THE CHURCH IN ORDER TO STRESS THE PIETY OF CRUSADING AND TO ENCOURAGE OTHERS TO TAKE UP THE CROSS.

greater influence on events than their relatively small numerical strength might suggest.

Throughout the thirteenth century, losses in the Holy Land and the decline in pious donations meant that the order was less able to commit to military ventures in the West, a situation compounded by the fact that the Spanish sought their help against various Christian enemies.

OTHER MILITARY ORDERS

The Templar presence was less prominent in areas of the Iberian Peninsula outside Portugal and Aragon. The kings of Castile preferred to use military orders such as the Knights of Santiago, the Knights of Alcantara, and the Knights of Calatrava. Preference for the locally based orders arose because they were less likely suddenly to go to the aid of the Christians in the East and withdraw their forces from Spain. Local orders could mobilize just as quickly, could spend long months on campaign, and their entire resources could be used to aid the Spanish cause. Use of these smaller orders had its drawbacks, however, for they had far fewer resources and they were unable to act independently.

THE CATHAR HERESY

The brutal Albigensian Crusade, the war against the Cathar communities in the Languedoc-Rousillon area of the south of France, was triggered by the murder of the papal legate, Peter de Castlenau, on January 14, 1208. He was allegedly killed by a vassal of Count Raymond IV of Toulouse, who was a supporter of the Cathar faith. Two months later the pope used the murder of his legate as an excuse to call a crusade against the Cathars, who he claimed were a far greater threat to the Christian Church than all the armies of Islam.

The Cathars were dualists—they believed that a good god had created spirit and an evil god had made the earth and everything in it. Everything material was therefore the product of the evil god, and salvation lay in releasing yourself from the bounds of the flesh. Like the Templars, they believed that Jesus was a divinely inspired man who had come to reveal the truth and that his initiatory teaching had been passed to John the Evangelist. The teaching had subsequently come to the Cathars in the only religious book they revered, *The Secret Gospel of John* or *The Gospel of Love*. The Cathars rejected all the Catholic sacraments. The consolamentum, a ritual laying on of hands, was their one and only sacrament, which an initiate took to become a perfectus. Preparation for the consolamentum usually took three years, after which the individual lived according to a set of strict rules, abstaining from sexual relations and not eating meat or by-products of the flesh such as milk or eggs, although they did eat fish. An ordinary believer could take the consolamentum on his or her deathbed which they believed broke the cycle of reincarnation that held them prisoner. The Cathars had no need of the Catholic Church to save their souls, for they believed that hell was in the present, here on earth, and not in the hereafter. They also committed the cardinal sin of refusing to recognize the authority of the pope. Their liberal attitude was a constant and growing threat to the power, influence, and income of the Church, a situation the pope could not tolerate.

The people of the Languedoc were known for their tolerance toward other cultures: a large Jewish population inhabited many of the towns and cities, and the proximity to Moorish Spain led to the absorption of Islamic ideas. The Catholic Church in the area was in a deplorable state. Church buildings were falling down and the corrupt clergy were leading a profligate lifestyle, more interested in the profit they could reap from their flock than in saving souls.

In an attempt to return the lapsed parishioners to the fold, a fanatical Spanish priest by the name of Dominic Guzman made his way to the Languedoc, where his prolonged preaching and proselytizing fell upon deaf ears. He then issued the following brutal warning:

> *For years I have brought you words of peace, I have preached, I have implored, I have wept. But, now as the common people say in Spain, if a blessing will not work, then it must be the stick. Now we shall stir up princes and bishops against you and they, alas, will call together nations and peoples and many will perish by the sword. Towers will be destroyed, walls overturned, and you will be reduced to slavery. Thus force will prevail where gentleness has failed.*

THE ALBIGENSIAN CRUSADE

In March 1208, Pope Innocent III issued a bull of anathema against the Cathars, condemning them all to death. He then called for a crusade, the only crusade in which Christian fought against Christian. Papal representatives and clergymen accompanied the crusading army to ensure that all suspected heretics were tortured before being burned at the stake. In the early stages of the crusade, the night before the end of the siege of Béziers, in the southwest of what is now France, the leaders of the crusading army, aware that the majority of the citizens were Catholics, asked the papal legate, Arnauld Aimery, for his advice on how they should identify their fellow Christians if the city fell. The reply they received was to "Show mercy neither to order, nor to age, nor to sex—Cathar or Catholic—kill them all ... God will know his own when they get to him!"

All volunteers for the forthcoming crusade were given absolution for their sins, past, present, and future. In return they had to serve for 40 days, in which time—under the auspices of the papacy—they pillaged, raped, murdered, and expropriated the property of anyone declared a heretic. Despite the fact that this was an official crusade,

---

PERFECTI AND CREDENTES

PERFECTUS (PLURAL PERFECTI) IS A CORRUPTION OF THE TERM HERETICUS PERFECTUS, GIVEN TO THE CATHARS BY THEIR CRITICS. IT REFERRED TO THOSE WHO HAD TAKEN THE CONSOLAMENTUM. THE ORDINARY BELIEVERS WERE KNOWN AS THE CREDENTES, AND INCLUDED BOTH SEXES. THE PERFECTI MINISTERED TO THE CREDENTES, WHO GREETED THEM WITH THE MELIORAMENTUM OR MELHORER. THE BELIEVER BOWED THREE TIMES TO THE PERFECTUS AND SAID, "PRAY TO GOD TO MAKE A GOOD CHRISTIAN OF ME, AND BRING ME TO A GOOD END."

THE POPULACE OF CARCASSONNE LEAVING THE CITY AFTER ITS CAPTURE BY THE CRUSADING ARMY UNDER SIMON DE MONTFORT. THE INHABITANTS WERE SPARED BUT FORCED TO LEAVE WEARING NOTHING BUT THEIR UNDERCLOTHES, AND HAD TO LEAVE THEIR PROPERTY TO THE MERCY OF THE CRUSADERS.

neither the Knights Templar nor the Knights Hospitaller took part. The Templars' involvement extended to little more than the collection of a "hearth tax" of three pence, imposed by the pope to pay the costs of the crusade.

The reasons given for both military orders' distinct lack of enthusiasm to fight fellow Christians are somewhat unconvincing. Both claimed that their holdings in the province were unsuitable for use in warfare; they were for agricultural and commercial purposes only, understaffed, unfortified, and not garrisoned for military use, making them ineffective as bases or defensive strong points. The knights also claimed that the deeds of donation for these estates specifically forbade their use for any warlike activity. The nobles who donated the lands in support of the Templars in the Languedoc also supported the Cathars, which may explain in part why the Knights of the Templar Order were reluctant to take part in the crusade. The Templars did not participate in the crusade, but they

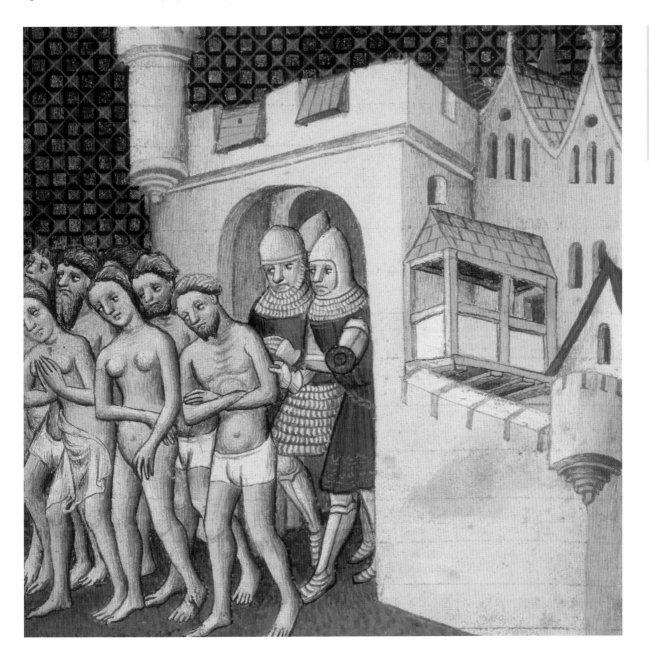

MONGOLS BESIEGING A CITADEL.
INITIALLY THE MONGOLS USED ONLY
MOUNTED ARCHERS IN BATTLE, BUT
SOON DEVELOPED THE USE OF THE
MANGONEL (STONE THROWER),
CATAPULT, AND SIEGE LADDERS.

were involved in assisting the knights who actively defended the Cathars against the crusading armies when they fought on the side of King Pedro II of Aragon in his attack on Simon de Montfort, the leader of the Albigensian Crusade. In the records of the Inquisition there is a remarkable correspondence between the leading Knights Templar in the area and those of the leading Cathar families, suggesting some form of familial loyalty was in force, for this was an area where many Rex Deus families had settled. Cathars fleeing from the crusaders were often given shelter by the Templars, who allowed their burial in consecrated ground, in direct contravention of the papal directive. This led to the obscene rite of disinterment of the Cathar cadavers, which were tried on charges of heresy at the behest of the Inquisition and found guilty as charged. The putrefying corpses were then ritually burned at the stake.

EASTERN EUROPE

Compared with the rest of Europe, the frontier region of Eastern Europe was underpopulated and undercultivated. One very efficient way of populating the empty land was through donations to the monastic and military orders. Colonization meant increased wealth and prosperity for the landowner and was the main reason for encouraging the orders into the area. The knights could be used as protectors for the proselytizing monks and the new converts, who were prime targets for attack by the local pagans. They raided pagan territory, taking booty and prisoners, in whose conversion they could then play a part.

The Templars' role here was very different from the one they played in the West. They had come to the area some considerable time after their foundation, and were relatively unknown in northeastern Europe before the 1220s. The donors of frontier land declared that they were making the gift in order to help in the fight against the Saracens. However, by helping the religious orders who were closely connected with the Holy War, many donors believed they could gain absolution.

From the late twelfth century, the Templars began to receive donations in the German Empire; in Bohemia and

> ## THE MONGOLS
>
> THE MONGOLS WERE A NOMADIC PEOPLE FROM NORTH-CENTRAL ASIA WHO, IN THE THIRTEENTH CENTURY UNDER GENGHIS KHAN, BUILT ONE OF THE WORLD'S LARGEST EMPIRES, STRETCHING FROM CHINA TO THE RIVER DANUBE IN EUROPE, AND INTO PERSIA (IRAN). INITIALLY THEIR TROOPS WERE COMPRISED OF MOUNTED ARCHERS, BUT BEFORE LONG THEY WERE BESIEGING CITIES USING MANGONELS (STONE THROWERS), CATAPULTS, LADDERS, AND BURNING OIL. EVENTUALLY, CONTINUOUS INTERNAL DISPUTES LED TO THE EMPIRE'S DECLINE.

Moravia most donations of land went to the Hospitallers and Teutonic Knights, with the Templars only receiving their first donation in 1230. Their role in Bohemia was not as warriors but principally to encourage the colonization of the area. They also received donations in Hungary after the 1160s, but these were of limited importance.

MONGOL INCURSIONS INTO EASTERN EUROPE

In 1241, the Mongols attacked Hungary, and the Templars played a leading role in the ensuing battle. The king of Croatia, his archbishop, and the Templar Master James of Montreal took action. They rushed into the fray, but were heavily outnumbered and—although their losses were fewer than those of the Mongols—they were forced to withdraw. When the Hungarians finally joined the battle, the Templars again launched an attack but were forced to retreat. The king of Croatia and the archbishop barely escaped with their lives; the Templar Master and the army were slaughtered. Poland was also attacked by the Mongols in 1241, and Templar possessions there were devastated. These battles were defensive in nature and were not part of a Holy War.

Substantial donations of land continued to come to the Templars, mostly on frontiers within Christian territory and on underdeveloped land within the region, although, in many cases, their presence was symbolic rather than strategic. In both the Iberian Peninsula and Eastern Europe the Templars often acted as representatives of landowners, custodians who protected it from any would-be invaders, creating wealth for all and raising much-needed funds for the support of their fellow knights in the Holy Land.

commercial activities
of the templar order

In the early part of the twelfth century, Europe was a conglomeration of squabbling feudal fiefdoms, baronies, counties, and kingdoms. Long-distance trade was almost nonexistent except by sea, and centered on the cities of Venice, Genoa, and Pisa, which all exploited their geographical position to trade with the Islamic and Byzantine Empires. However, there was a slow but steady improvement in the wealth of northern Europe in the early twelfth century, and a growing trade developed in goods, such as woollen cloth and timber, which was exchanged for more exotic goods from the East, mainly silk and spices. At the time of the foundation of the Templars, most towns were small and virtually powerless; however, with the advent of the Knights Templar all this changed dramatically.

LONG-DISTANCE TRADE

Long-distance overland trade was uneconomical because of the heavy tolls imposed on goods in transit by feudal lords. Travelers carrying goods or large sums of money were also at risk of being attacked by brigands, robbed, and beaten. With the rise of the Templar Order and its rapidly increasing landholdings, long distance travel became safer and more feasible. The order's estates scattered throughout Europe gave the Templars bases from which they could protect the pilgrimage routes that were also used for trade, thus their contribution to the peace and safety of the routes they policed enabled the merchants to transport their goods in comparative safety over longer distances.

These activities led to the development and growth of large regional markets, which stimulated trade still further. Merchants were encouraged to take their business to the markets at Troyes in the county of Champagne, for the counts of Champagne were sufficiently independent of their nominal overlords

(the king of France and the duke of Burgundy) to ignore any royal trade restrictions. Occasionally, commercial privileges given to the Templars themselves caused disputes, as at Provins in the county of Champagne, where they were granted rights to levy tolls on certain produce and the merchants claimed that the order was exploiting this privilege unfairly. However, other powerful nobles soon followed the example set by the counts of Champagne, and long-distance trade began to develop under the watchful eyes of the Templars. In England the order was granted the right to hold weekly fairs and annual markets at many of the commanderies, which attracted much-needed trade and considerably boosted local economies.

The major Templar innovation that reinforced the growth of trade and which ultimately brought about a change in the balance of power between the feudal lords and the towns was the creation of a complex and highly efficient banking system.

TEMPLAR BANKING

It is impossible for a high level of growth in trade to flourish without an efficient financial infrastructure to support it. The Templars now took on the role of international bankers, offering their services to the newly emerging merchant class. They had become adept at organizing the safe transport of gold and money across Europe to finance their activities in the Holy Land, and using a technique learned from their Muslim adversaries, the "note of hand," they arranged financial transfers from one part of Europe to another. The traveler deposited money with the Templar treasurer at one commanderie, a note of hand was issued, which was then presented to the treasurer at the traveler's destination. The amount stated on the note was then paid to

LEFT: THE PROSPEROUS REPUBLIC OF VENICE, WHICH USED ITS PRIME MARITIME POSITION TO FOSTER TRADE AND FOUND A VIRTUAL EMPIRE.

RIGHT: A TEMPLAR TREASURER. THE BANKING SYSTEM DEVELOPED BY THE ORDER SPURRED A RAPID GROWTH IN TRADE.

the holder, thus avoiding the necessity for personally carrying large sums of money. The Templars also developed the banker's draft and the precursor of the modern credit card.

A ROYAL TREASURY

The first European monarch to benefit from the Templar banking activities was King Louis VII of France, who received a loan that almost bankrupted the order. By the late twelfth century, during the reign of King Philippe II, the Templars

had in effect become the royal treasury. The kings of Aragon borrowed heavily from them, as did King John of England, whose father, King Henry II, had used the order as bankers in Jerusalem, where he accumulated funds in preparation for participating in the crusades. From 1229, Henry III of England had as royal almoner a Templar, who became Keeper of the Wardrobe, thereby controlling the king's personal treasury. Henry used the Paris Temple as a depository for the English crown jewels from 1261 "until further notice," which came in 1264, when he used them as security on a loan for money he needed to pursue further campaigns against the barons who were rebelling against him.

In England the treasury was run by royal officials as part of the royal household; in France the order acted as the royal treasury, the treasurer of the Paris Temple being the *de facto* royal treasurer, banking tax revenues and administering payments to royal officials and soldiers. In 1295, the king of France set up his own royal treasury, but in 1303, some of its functions were transferred back to the

KING LOUIS VII (c.1120-80) OF FRANCE RECEIVING THE PILGRIM'S STAFF FROM POPE EUGENIUS III IN ST DENIS IN 1147. THE TEMPLARS AND HOSPITALLERS BOTH ADVANCED HIM LOANS ENABLING HIM TO REMAIN IN THE HOLY LAND DURING THE SECOND CRUSADE.

Temple. Thus the financial skills of the order became essential to the smooth running of France.

The papacy also relied heavily on the Templars for its financial needs. As early as 1163, the order was acting as banker to Pope Alexander III, and it was used again by Pope Innocent III when, prior to the Fourth Crusade, he reorganized the way the crusades were financed. Taxes levied on the clergy for the purpose of funding the campaigns in the East were deposited with the Templars and Hospitallers, who were responsible for the safe transport of funds to the Holy Land. In 1220, Pope Honorius III entrusted his financial contribution to the Fifth Crusade to a Templar and Hospitaller, claiming that "there was no one he could trust better."

Charging interest on loans was forbidden in the medieval era, with the exception of the Jewish moneylenders. Anyone breaking this law was charged with usury. The Knights Templar came up with an ingenious solution to overcome this. Charging rent on property was normal practice, so instead of levying interest on the loans they made, the Templars charged "rent." This was chargeable at the time the loan was made and added to the capital. In this way they avoided having to make an appearance before the courts on a charge of usury. Some loans from southern France included a clause that stated that if there was depreciation in the value of the coin between the date the loan was made and the repayment, then the borrower had to add a fixed sum to the capital to compensate the lender. Hiding the interest charge under the guise of recompense for depreciation was, in many cases, yet another means of disguising the usurious nature of the loan.

The Templars quickly rose to be the wealthiest financial institution in the Christian world at that time. Their moneylending activities were not restricted to the upper classes, they lent to everyone: to merchants, to the nobility, to bishops to finance church-building projects, and to princes, emperors, and kings to finance state building programs, wars, and crusades.

Pilgrims and crusaders could be away from home for many years, and the safest place to deposit their valuables during their absence (including documents such as wills

and other items) was with the Templars, either at their local administration centers or the provincial headquarters in London or Paris.

There is only one documented account of a complaint about the Templars' mishandling of money. Jean de Joinville was a pious man, a noble from a wealthy family in Champagne, and a crusader. He deposited a large sum of money with the order in Acre soon after his arrival in 1250. When he sent his representative to withdraw funds from his account, the Templar treasurer denied all knowledge of the deposit. However, Jean made a complaint, which at first was disbelieved, but four days later, after an anxious wait, he was told that his money had been found. The Templar treasurer was relocated. While no other such complaints are documented, the Templars nonetheless gained a reputation for greed, which may have arisen from similar incidents.

The Knights Templars' protection of the trade routes, their financial acumen, and the economic stability that arose as a result meant that power dramatically shifted from the feudal barons to the emergent mercantile bourgeoisie in the towns and cities, a change that ultimately led to the development of capitalism.

TEMPLAR INDUSTRY

The Templar's own wealth came from a diverse number of ventures with one purpose in mind—to support their comrades in the East. Much of it came from donations to the order, but the Templars also gained a vast income from their independent commercial pursuits. Their agricultural activities were not restricted to the cultivation and use of the land but also in processing the end product. Mills were needed to grind the grain from the corn, and were an important means of generating income.

Where land was unsuitable for cultivation, it could be used for pasture. The Templars owned large flocks of sheep both in Yorkshire, England, and in the Iberian Peninsula in Europe, although the size of their flocks never equaled that of the Cistercians. Wool production led to the order's involvement in cloth manufacture, and here the water mills demonstrated their usefulness yet again. The process of "fulling"—the strenuous task of pounding and washing the cloth—that had previously been done by hand was the first industry to be mechanized. Large wooden hammers powered by the water mill were now used to pound the cloth. The Templars owned two fulling mills in England.

The Templars not only had substantial strategic investments in land and agricultural pursuits but also invested in basic industries, such as stone quarrying, which provided the essential ingredients for the considerable expansion in lay and ecclesiastical building that changed the face of Europe in the twelfth century. Their industrial activities were not limited to quarrying; they also mined for coal and metal ores, and built smelting factories to process the ore before using it in manufacturing agricultural tools and, of course, arms and armor. The Templars made the best use of the local products wherever they had holdings, whether in Europe or the East. At Castle Pilgrim in Palestine they had a distillery to produce salt from the seawater, and at the village of as-Sumairiya in the kingdom of Jerusalem they owned a glass factory. King Henry III of England gave them two forges in London, which they rented out because it made better economic sense to install tenants than to run the forges themselves. The order had a substantial investment in viniculture; for example at La Rochelle (their principal port on the Atlantic coast) they owned several vineyards producing wine not only for their own consumption but also for export in their own ships, something that is well documented in the port records.

GUARANTEE OF SAFE PASSAGE

The twelfth-century version of the "package-tour industry" arose from the actions of the Order of the Knights Templar. Pilgrimage in the medieval era was long, arduous, and expensive for the pilgrim, and extremely profitable for the Church, innkeepers, ferrymen, and others en route. However, the fear of extortion and robbery made the travelers wary of carrying large sums of money. Templar protection meant that pilgrims or traders could travel along the major routes of Europe in comparative safety. Before embarking on his pilgrimage, the traveler approached the master of his local Templar commanderie, where he deposited enough funds to cover his return journey. This included the actual travel costs, accommodation, and ancillary costs that would be incurred, such as alms-giving. The Templar treasurer then gave the pilgrim a receipt in the form of a coded chit that could also be used as a means of exchange. At each stopping point on the journey, or where alms or offerings had to be made, the pilgrim gave his chit to the local Templar treasurer who then recoded it and returned it to its owner. The outstanding dues were paid to the creditor by the Templar representative. When the pilgrimage was

ABOVE LEFT: A MEDIEVAL SHEEP SHEARER AT WORK. WOOL PRODUCTION WAS ONE OF THE AGRICULTURAL PURSUITS FOLLOWED BY THE BROTHERS, THOUGH COMPARED TO THE CISTERCIANS THE TEMPLARS' OUTPUT OF WOOL WAS SMALL.

RIGHT: THE TEMPLAR MILL AT DA'UK WHERE THE LAND WAS SO FLAT THE WATERWHEELS HAD TO REVOLVE HORIZONTALLY.

over, the pilgrim went to the treasurer who had issued his chit, which was checked. If it was in credit the pilgrim would receive a refund; if there was a debit balance he received a bill. In operating the pilgrimage trade in this way, the Templars became forerunners of the modern package-tour industry, and the coded chit was a medieval precursor of the modern credit card.

THE PILGRIMAGE TO COMPOSTELA

Going on a pilgrimage to Compostela in Spain was second only in spiritual importance to making the trip to the Holy City of Jerusalem, and far more important than embarking on a journey to Rome. The pilgrims traveling to Compostela in northwestern Spain even had their own "guidebook"—the Benedictine tract *Codex Callextinus*, also known as the *Liber*

RIGHT: A STATUE OF JAMES THE GREAT FOUND ON TOP OF THE HOLY GATE AT THE CATHEDRAL OF COMPOSTELA SHOWING HIM WEARING A TYPICAL PILGRIM'S HAT BEARING THE SCALLOP SHELL AND CARRYING THE PILGRIM'S STAFF. THE UPPER CATHEDRAL AT COMPOSTELA IS DEDICATED TO JAMES THE GREAT, AND SUPPOSEDLY HOLDS HIS RELICS, WHILE THE LOWER CHURCH IS DEDICATED TO JAMES THE LESS.

LEFT: A MEDIEVAL CALENDAR ILLUSTRATING THE RETURN OF THE PILGRIMS FROM SANTIAGO DE COMPOSTELA. THE MAJORITY OF PILGRIMS WHO MADE THE ARDUOUS JOURNEY ON FOOT ALONG THE WAY OF ST. JAMES TRAVELED FROM FRANCE.

Sancti Jacobi, or *Book of St. James*—which would have been read to them by the local priest. This document, which describes the route to the shrine of St. James at Compostela from any part of Europe, is still extant. One folio contains instructions on how to avoid thieves and dishonest innkeepers; another has lists of the appropriate prayers and hymns for the pilgrimage.

It may seem strange that this journey was undertaken to Compostela, an obscure and relatively inaccessible part of Spain, and not to Rome, the heart of the Christian community where both Paul and Peter supposedly died. Outwardly Compostela is associated with James the Great, the son of Zebedee, one of Jesus' disciples, who is said to have been martyred at Jerusalem in 44 CE. A tomb found at Padrón near the present town of Compostela is said to have been supernaturally revealed as that of James the Great. A church erected over the tomb was destroyed by fire in 997. Construction of the present cathedral began in 1078, and it houses the reliquary containing his remains; esoterically, however, it is dedicated to James the Less, whose head is contained in a silver bust with a jeweled and gilt-enameled face. In the cathedral guidebook this reliquary is described in the following terms, "The most important silver bust is that of St. James the Less. The cranium of this saint, the younger brother of St. James the Great, was brought from Jerusalem to Braga in the twelfth century." In fact, James the Less and James the Great, although both Apostles, were not related. The crypt or Lower Church was used by the Rex Deus families who venerated this important reliquary, which they believed to be that of James the Just, or James the Less, brother of Jesus, the first bishop and leader of the Church in Jerusalem after the crucifixion. The pilgrimage to Compostela was undoubtedly the most significant single commercial enterprise in Europe, and the most lucrative.

TRANSFORMATION OF EUROPE

The Order of the Knights Templar exerted a transformative influence on the whole of Europe, yet many modern Church historians still accuse the order of being formed of "illiterate" knights. These so-called illiterates overcame the language barriers that would otherwise hinder their activities by

developing a highly sophisticated code as a method of communication. Furthermore, in the Holy Land, the Templars developed respect for Islam and used the knowledge and ideas gained from their Muslim adversaries for the benefit of the people of Europe. Among the technological advances that the order brought to Europe were the principles of stellar navigation, considerable knowledge in the fields of medicine and surgery (including mouth-to-mouth resuscitation, herbal medicine, and healing skills), and mathematics. Prior to the Templars, the concept of chivalry was unknown to Western Europe; this idea originated from the supposedly "heathen" Saracens, who, in most respects, were far more cultured than their Western adversaries.

organization and beliefs

THE TEMPLARS' ORGANIZATION WAS OUTWARDLY VERY SIMILAR TO THE OTHER MILITARY ORDERS, FOR THEY LIVED ACCORDING TO A MONASTIC RULE. WHAT MADE THE TEMPLARS UNIQUE WAS THE HERETICAL BELIEF SYSTEM THAT INFLUENCED THEIR ACTIONS THROUGHOUT THEIR EXISTENCE.

Church of The Holy

The head of the Templar Order was the Grand Master. He was based at the headquarters in the East with his senior officers who bore responsibility for specific matters of governance. The county of Tripoli and the principality of Antioch in the kingdom of Jerusalem each had its own master, who was subject to the authority of the Grand Master. Europe was divided into provinces, each under a provincial commander, who commanded lesser officials who oversaw the separate houses. The brothers in the Holy Land kept in touch with what was happening to their brothers in Europe via a system of chapter meetings.

The order comprised three categories: knights, sergeants, and priests. The knights formed the heavy cavalry. The sergeants were divided into two groups: one, drawn from the commoners and occasionally the nobility, fought alongside the knights, often on horseback; the other was made up of the working brothers, who saw to the smooth running of the Templar houses, attending to practical and domestic needs as well as overseeing agricultural activities. The priests were the only ordained members of the order and were forbidden to fight. They were viewed with a degree of derision by the knights, for they never dirtied their hands either by fighting or maintaining the estates.

THE GRAND MASTER

The Grand Master was elected for life. On the death of a Grand Master, the Grand Commander, who was the senior administrative officer, consulted with the chief military officer and the commanders of Jerusalem, Tripoli, and Antioch to set the date for the election. Thirteen electors, eight knights, four sergeants, and a chaplain, were selected by a complex procedure, supposedly designed to allow God to take a hand in the process. Thirteen was also held to be symbolic of Jesus and the 12 disciples. A member who spent time serving in the East was usually chosen in preference to

GRAND MASTERS OF THE TEMPLE	
c.1119–c.1136	HUGHES DE PAYEN
c.1136–c.1149	ROBERT DE CRAON
c.1149–c.1152	EVERARD DES BARRES
c.1152–1153	BERNARD DE TREMELAY
1153–1156	ANDRE DE MONTBARD
1156–1169	BERTRAND DE BLANCHFORT
1169–1171	PHILIP DE MILLY
c.1171–1179	ODO DE ST. AMAND
1181–1184	ARNOLD OF TORROJA
1185–1189	GERARD DE RIDEFORT
1191–c.1193	ROBERT DE SABLE
1194–1200	GILBERT ERAIL
1201–1209	PHILIP DE PLESSIS
1210–c.1219	GUILLAUME DE CHARTRES
1219–c.1232	PETER DE MONTAIGU
c.1232–1244	ARMAND DE PERIGORD
c.1244–c.1247	RICHARD DE BURES
c.1247–1250	GUILLAUME DE SONNAC
1250–1256	REGINALD DE VICHIERS
1256–1273	THOMAS BERARD
1273–1291	GUILLAUME DE BEAUJEU
1291–c.1293	THIBAUD GAUDIN
c.1293–1314	JACQUES DE MOLAY

one from the West. Two exceptions to this lifetime dedicated to service were Everard des Barres, who eventually resigned to retire to a Cistercian monastery, and Philip de Milly, who tendered his resignation to return to a secular life. The election of the new Grand Master was taken very seriously and took place at the order's headquarters, initially in Jerusalem, then at Acre, and later, after the loss of the Holy Land, on Cyprus. From the statutes of 1186, when the election rules were formalized, we can discern that it was deemed far more important to elect the best man for the job than to select an unsuitable leader in haste. However, the candidates for the title of Grand Master would have been carefully chosen from the inner circle, drawn exclusively from the Rex Deus members of the order.

CHAPTER MEETINGS

Chapter meetings were convened for the discussion of business and to hear legal cases, both in Europe and the

THE CHURCH OF THE HOLY SEPULCHRE IN JERUSALEM, WHICH IS SUPPOSEDLY BUILT ON THE SITE OF JESUS' TOMB. THE EARLIEST ROUND CHURCH TO ACHIEVE RENOWN THROUGHOUT CHRISTENDOM, IT IS CLAIMED AS A MODEL FOR SIMILAR CHURCHES IN EUROPE BY THE KNIGHTS TEMPLAR.

Holy Land. The general chapter, overseen by the Grand Master, appointed leading officials, made decisions as to which brothers were no longer fit for active service and should be sent back to Europe, heard disciplinary cases, and dealt with "any other business."

A provincial chapter meeting, presided over by the provincial master and which all the heads of the individual houses would attend, was held annually. The procedures followed those of the general chapter, but any cases too difficult for the provincial chapter to deal with were referred to the general chapter in the East.

EUROPEAN PROVINCES

European provinces developed as the order acquired more property. The official in overall charge was the commander. One house in the province was chosen as a center of administration, at which the treasure and records for that district were stored; in England this was in London and in northern France it was Paris. The provincial master validated documents with his own seal, which was usually of a standard design showing the Church of the Holy Sepulchre on the French seals and the Agnus Dei, the Lamb of God, on the English ones. Seals from other provinces had their own symbol: the German provincial master's seal varied, with one in the late thirteenth century showing Christ's head and another at the end of that century showing an eagle.

THE COMMANDERIE

The commanderie was the local administrative center. In the papal bull *Omne Datum Optimum* of 1139, it was granted the right to have its own chapel as long as it was for the sole use of the order. The commander was the equivalent to the lord of the manor, and held the responsibility of looking after his tenants. He was the local law-enforcement officer, who saw that justice was done, ensured that rents were paid, and that donations were collected. It was his responsibility to accept all donations of money to the order and to send all surplus funds to the provincial headquarters from where they would be forwarded to the Holy Land.

Commanderies in southern France were usually fortified, particularly on routes that were policed and protected by the Templars. The occupants of the commanderie comprised: knights; sergeants, both military and nonmilitary, who

LEFT: THE FORTIFIED CITY OF LA COUVERTOIRADE WAS EN ROUTE FOR COASTAL PORTS AND THE HOLY LAND. A FARMING CENTER, IT SUPPLIED THE ORDER WITH GRAIN, SHEEP, AND WARHORSES.

ABOVE: A CHAPTER MEETING OF THE TEMPLAR ORDER AT THEIR HEADQUARTERS IN PARIS. THESE MEETINGS WERE GENERALLY HELD ANNUALLY AT THE PROVINCIAL HEADQUARTERS.

worked as carpenters, smiths, and stonemasons, and who were responsible for animal husbandry; chaplains, who saw to the spiritual needs of the others; associates, both male and female, who took the role of spiritual warriors and prayed for the order; pensioners sent home from the East; and both free and bonded servants. The knights, sergeants, and chaplains all took vows of poverty, chastity, and obedience; the associate members were exempted from taking the vows. Few of the occupants of the Western commanderies fought in the crusades against the Muslims.

THE STATUS OF KNIGHTHOOD

Any knight who was unmarried and free, with no connection to any other religious house, was entitled to apply to join the Knights Templar. A knight was a fully trained professional warrior who fought either on horseback using a lance or sword, or occasionally on foot using a battleaxe or bow and arrows. During the twelfth century, new fighting techniques, such as the cavalry charge with couched lance, elevated the status of knighthood, making its attainment more difficult. Long hours of training were required, which restricted entry to those with the time and the money. Chain mail and swords improved in quality, and armor became more sophisticated, adding to the cost. A knightly culture began to develop in response to adverse criticism by the Church, who accused knights of being mindless and bloodthirsty butchers, or from merchants, who condemned them for their lack of practicality and business sense (despite the fact that many Templar knights held positions of power within governments).

The Templars were often accused of being haughty and proud, but they simply saw this as exhibiting their sense of self-esteem, for as knights they regarded themselves as being born to a higher social status than the merchants, who they believed lied and cheated in order to make money. Eventually, knighthood was seen as a sign of nobility. By the thirteenth century, to be a knight within the order you had to have already attained knighthood, be the son of a knight or the son of a knight's daughter, and to be of legitimate birth.

ADMISSION TO THE ORDER

The original Rule required a training period, but this was abandoned when heavy losses in the East necessitated rapid recruitment. An aspirant kept a lonely vigil in the chapel through the night, followed by an initiation ceremony at dawn. The novice was warned that life in the order was harsh, that he would have to follow orders without question, and that some of his work might be degrading. He had to be free of other commitments, be neither a serf nor married, and not owe a sum of money larger than he could pay. The candidate promised to give all his personal property to the order, live chastely, obey the Grand Master and the Rule, and work to help his colleagues conquer the Holy Land. He made his promises to God and Our Lady St. Mary. It is, however, unclear to which St. Mary he was swearing fealty.

In the twelfth and thirteenth centuries, the feminine began to come back into Catholicism with the rise of

Mariolatry, the veneration of the Virgin Mary. However, when Bernard of Clairvaux gave the Templars their Rule at the Council of Troyes, he was specific in his requirement that all members of the order make "Obedience to Bethany and the House of Mary and Martha"—in fact, he was telling them to swear obedience to the dynasty founded by Jesus and Mary Magdalene.

The achievements of the Templar Order in the brief 180-year period of their existence far outweigh those of any other military order of the time. An examination of their actions and beliefs raises the questions "What made the Templars so different from the other military orders?" and "How were they able to effect the transformations that affected nearly every inhabitant in Europe?" To begin to understand this, we need first to examine their spiritual and religious beliefs.

THE OUTER CIRCLE

The ordinary sergeants, craftsmen, and auxiliary members were staunch Catholics who followed the teaching of the Church without question. However, from the very beginning of the order, the founders and real leaders were gnostics and heretics who were almost certainly adept at the art of dissembling. Thus the majority of ordinary members followed a very different belief system from that of the inner circles, namely a traditional monastic life, as laid down in the sixth-century Rule of St. Benedict. Not every Templar house had its own chapel, but in those that did these brothers heard the whole divine office every day ("the hours" that took place on the first, third, sixth, and ninth hour), as well as compulsory additional services on feast days and holy days. If they were on campaign in the East or the Iberian Peninsula, or where they were unable to hear the hours, they were under a sacred obligation to say the Lord's Prayer a specific number of times.

The Statutes of the order set out the details of the day, beginning with the compulsory services, followed by the other regulations that governed the Templars' daily life. Brothers were enjoined to converse quietly and politely with each other; gambling, swearing, and getting drunk were forbidden. Anyone who was repeatedly inebriated

THE TEMPLARS' DAY ACCORDING TO THE RULE OF THE TEMPLE
BASED UPON THE RULE OF ST. BENEDICT

TIME	SERVICE IN CHAPEL (OR HALL)	EXPLANATORY NOTES
AT NIGHT	MATINS	THIS WAS THE FIRST SERVICE OF THE DAY AND WOULD TAKE PLACE AT 2 A.M. IN THE WINTER AND JUST BEFORE FIRST LIGHT IN THE SUMMER. THE SERVICE WOULD BE SHORTER IN THE SUMMER, AND LONGER IN THE WINTER. ON SUNDAY, IT COULD LAST FOR UP TO TWO HOURS.
c. 6 A.M.	PRIME	THE DAY WAS DIVIDED INTO NINE "HOURS," AND READINGS WOULD TAKE PLACE AT REGULAR INTERVALS DURING THE DAY. PRIME IS SO CALLED BECAUSE IT TAKES PLACE AT THE FIRST "HOUR" OF THE DAY. MASS WOULD FOLLOW AFTER PRIME, OR ALTERNATIVELY, THIS WOULD BE HELD AFTER SEXT.
	MASS (OR AFTER SEXT)	
c. 9 A.M.	TERCE	TERCE TAKES PLACE AT THE THIRD "HOUR" OF THE DAY.
c. 12 NOON	SEXT	SEXT IS THE SIXTH "HOUR" OF THE DAY, AFTER WHICH MASS WOULD BE HELD IF IT HAD NOT TAKEN PLACE AFTER PRIME. THE PERIOD AFTER SEXT WOULD BE THE TIME WHEN KNIGHTS CARRIED OUT THEIR TEMPORAL DUTIES WHICH, WHEN ON ACTIVE SERVICE, WOULD INCLUDE TENDING TO THEIR ARMS AND ARMOR. THIS WOULD BE FOLLOWED BY THE MAIN MEAL OF THE DAY.
	MASS (IF NOT HEARD EARLIER)	
c. 3 P.M.	NONES	NONES IS THE NINTH "HOUR" OF THE DAY. VESPERS OR VIGILS FOR THE DEAD MIGHT FOLLOW.
	VESPERS FOR THE DEAD	
	VIGILS FOR THE DEAD	
DUSK	VESPERS	VESPERS IS THE LAST SERVICE OF DAYLIGHT, FOLLOWING WHICH SUPPER WOULD BE EATEN
NIGHT	COMPLINE	COMPLINE TAKES PLACE AFTER SUNDOWN, AFTER WHICH KNIGHTS RETIRE.

GENERAL NOTES:

1. DURING PERIODS OF FASTING THERE WAS ONLY ONE MEAL A DAY AT 3 P.M. OR 4 P.M.

2. ORDERS WERE HANDED OUT TO BROTHERS BEFORE THE "HOURS" SERVICE IN CHAPEL.

3. CHAPTER MEETINGS WERE HELD ON SUNDAYS AND AT CHRISTMAS, EASTER, AND PENTECOST.

could be asked to leave the order, although the Templars did have a reputation for drunkenness, and in common parlance it was an insult to be accused of "drinking like a Templar." Fraternizing with women was forbidden—anyone found caught in the act faced being dismissed from the order or, if he was allowed to stay, he would be permanently barred from holding any responsible position. The Templars' oath of chastity meant that any form of sex was forbidden.

THE INNER CIRCLE

The founders of the order formed a tightly knit inner circle from which the leadership was always chosen. French researchers and writers George Cagger and Jean Robin state:

The Order was constituted of seven "exterior" circles dedicated to the minor mysteries, and of three "inner" circles corresponding to the initiation into the great mysteries ... this "nucleus" was composed of 70 Templars.

The religious beliefs of the knights within the order would have covered a wide spectrum. Within the outer circles of the mainstream believers were hidden concentric graded circles, each of which professed hidden beliefs and a level of knowledge according to the degree that they had attained within the order. Rex Deus members had the right of birth to enter into the higher echelons of the three inner circles, and from time to time other candidates from the outer circles who were considered suitable were admitted.

Only knights who proved themselves reliable and trustworthy were entrusted with the dangerous knowledge that could have provoked charges of heresy. The nucleus of 70 continued to be made up solely of members of the Rex Deus dynasty who had reached the highest degree of initiation, keeping control safely in their hands.

The members of the nucleus maintained an active interest in pursuing research into esoteric and religious matters that arose from the combined roots of the Rex Deus traditions and the scrolls discovered under the Temple Mount shortly after the order's foundation in 1118. Unlike the simple Christians who made up the rank and file of the Knights Templar order, these scholars did not spend time seeking eternal salvation, but used the sacred knowledge they gained for the direct benefit of the communities in which they lived.

TEMPLAR SEALS

Evidence of the Templar Order's gnostic and dualist beliefs can be found in the large number of seals that are still in existence. The Grand Master's seal was always double-sided. On one side was the Church of the Holy Sepulchre, which was in fact a depiction of the al-Aqsa mosque, the building under which the original nine knights made their excavations; on the other was an image of the two brothers on one horse. Contrary to popular belief this was not a demonstration of the knights' poverty but a coded reference to their dualistic beliefs. The Grand Master had another seal that he used on the documents that were "confidential" or "top secret"—the Abraxus, which is unarguably gnostic and whose roots can be found in ancient Greek hermeticism. The ancient symbol of wisdom, the serpent eating its own tail, is occasionally used with the Abraxus. Two other seals (which appear to be from mainstream Christianity) show the Paschal Lamb (the Agnus Dei) carrying a cross—not the cross associated with Jesus, however, but the long-stemmed cross symbolic of John the Baptist.

Other dualistic seals show two brothers behind an escarboucle, an almond-shaped shield: a carving of this is on the west front of Chartres, Rheims, and Amiens cathedrals. A carving of two brothers on one horse in Scotland's Rosslyn Chapel, which was built by Earl William St. Clair in the fifteenth century as a memorial to the Templars, is disguised as Bartholomew Ladislaus Leslyn bringing Princess Margaret to Scotland to marry King Malcolm Canmore. There is a view that these enigmatic seals hide the heretical belief that Jesus had a twin brother, Thomas Didymus (Didymus is Greek for "twin"). The Gospel of Thomas found among the Nag Hammadi scrolls in Egypt opens with the statement that Thomas is Jesus' twin brother. The Templars' battle standard, the beauseant, bore a simple design in black and white—both this color scheme and their other habit of twinning their domains are further signs of their dualistic beliefs.

LEFT: A DEPICTION OF A PILGRIM, WEARING A TRADITIONAL HAT DISPLAYING THE SCALLOP SHELL AND CARRYING A STAFF, A TEMPLAR KNIGHT WITH THE RED CROSS ON A WHITE MANTLE, AND A HOSPITALLER KNIGHT WITH THE WHITE CROSS ON A BLACK MANTLE.

ABOVE: THE DOUBLE-SIDED SEAL OF THE GRAND MASTER REPRESENTED THE DUALISTIC BELIEFS OF THE ORDER. THE IMAGE OF TWO BROTHERS ON A HORSE WAS DISPLAYED ON ONE SIDE AND THE CHURCH OF THE HOLY SEPULCHRE ON THE OTHER.

Other symbols associated with the ancient wisdom were also used, such as the crescent moon, upon which Mary Magdalene or Mary the mother of Jesus is often shown standing, surrounded by five-pointed stars, both representations of the Babylonian goddess Ishtar and the principle of divine wisdom; the Star of the Sea, a term used in the litany of the Virgin Mary that was originally used in the litany of Ishtar; and the fleur-de-lis, the emblem of the Royal House of France that originated in ancient Egypt, and is a symbol of the Rex Deus families. These symbols were exhibited in plain sight for all to see but could only be understood by the initiated.

TEMPLAR RELICS

At their trial the Templars were accused of venerating a bearded head known as Baphomet. According to the Templar scholar, the late Guy Jourdan of Provence, the head of John the Baptist, for which Amiens Cathedral was built, is *la vrai tête Baphometique Templier* ("the true Baphometic head of the Templars"). Hugh Schonfield, the Dead Sea Scrolls scholar, applied the Atbash cipher (an esoteric code used by the Essenes to disguise the meaning of their scriptures) to the name Baphomet and found that it translates as "Sophia," the spiritual principle of Wisdom, which is usually associated with the ancient Greek or early Mesopotamian goddesses.

Idries Shah, author of *The Sufis*, claims that Baphomet is a corruption of the Arabic *abufihamet* (pronounced "bufhimat"), which translates as "Father of Understanding." Magnus Eliphas Levi, the nineteenth-century mystical writer, proposed that it should be spelled in reverse as TEM. OHP. AB, which he then interpreted as *Templi Hominum Pacis Omnium Abbas* or "Father of the Temple of Universal Peace Among Men."

The recurrent veneration of heads is certainly a part of surviving Templar tradition, and this includes the head of St. Euphemia of Chalcedon, a martyr from the fourth century. It is unclear whether the Templars had only the head of St. Euphemia or her whole body, or the relics of someone they believed to be her, for her relics are claimed to reside today at the Patriarchal Church of St. George in Istanbul. At the trial of the Templars, one witness described a silver reliquary containing the head of another saint that was allegedly kept at Nicosia in Cyprus and which, after the dissolution of the Templars, passed into the possession of the Knights Hospitaller in 1395, and was then kept at the Church of St. John at Rhodes. Another head discovered in the Paris Temple was identified as being female. It too was kept in a silver reliquary and given to the Hospitallers after 1314.

THE SHROUD OF TURIN

In 1203, a French crusader, Robert de Clari, described an object he had seen exhibited at the Church of My Lady St. Mary of Blachernae at Constantinople:

> ... where was kept the sidoine (shroud) in which Our Lord had been wrapped, which stood up straight every Friday so that the figure of Our Lord could plainly be seen there ... no one, either Greek or French, ever knew what became of this sidoine after the city was taken.

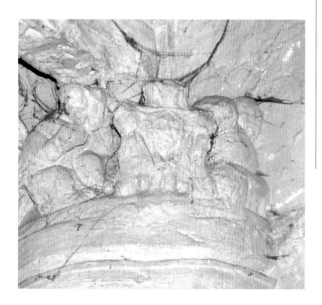

LEFT: A CARVING OF THE VEIL OF VERONICA, LOCATED IN THE SOUTH AISLE AT ROSSLYN CHAPEL. THIS SYMBOL IS ALSO KNOWN AS THE MANDYLION.

RIGHT: THE CHURCH OF ST. JOHN, RHODES, WHICH CONTAINS A SAINTLY TEMPLAR RELIC THAT PASSED INTO THE POSSESSION OF THE KNIGHTS HOSPITALLER.

The translation of the word "figure" could mean either "the face" or a "full-length drawing." Thus the Shroud of Turin could have been the Mandylion, a depiction of a bearded head on a cloth similar to the Veil of Veronica. The same persistent legend that neither was "made by the hand of man" pertains to them both and if the Shroud was folded and framed, as the historian and sidonologist Ian Wilson claims, then only the head would have been visible. In addition, the known and provable history of the

nephew of Geoffroi de Charney, who was martyred along with Jacques de Molay on the Isle des Javiaux in 1314. The de Charney family were related to the families of Brienne, de Joinville, and d'Anjou, as well as with the house of Burgundy. All were members of Rex Deus and some were involved in the sack of Constantinople (modern Istanbul) in 1204. The head of John the Baptist also came into the Templars' possession following the sack of Constantinople. Did the leaders of the order have foreknowledge of these

Mandylion matches the earlier missing history of the Shroud, with one small gap.

The first recorded public exhibition of the Shroud was in the mid-fourteenth century, at a small church at Lirey in the diocese of Troyes, an area of strong Templar influence in the twelfth and thirteenth centuries. Its owners, the de Charney family, were indisputably connected to the Templar Order, for Geoffrey de Charney, who died in 1356, was the

two relics? We can only speculate as to the answer to this question, but it is highly likely that through the traditions of the Rex Deus families the whereabouts of both were known. It is also possible that the face of Jesus depicted on the Shroud became linked with the Templar veneration of a bearded head. One such image that bears Rex Deus symbolism was found in Templecombe, in Somerset, England, and is now exhibited in the local church. This is generally believed to be the head of Jesus but the Rex Deus belief is that it is John the Baptist; the platter on which the head rests can be faintly discerned in the foreground. In the background can be seen depictions of the fleur-de-lys, indicating that he is part of the Rex Deus line. Other clues to Templar beliefs can be found in allegorical form in the sagas of the Holy Grail, a fascinating body of literary work that originated in the city of Troyes, in the county of Champagne. The first Grail romance was the story of Perceval, or *Le Conte del Graal*, written by Chrétien de Troyes for Philip, Count of Flanders, which circulated c.1190 in the form of an unfinished epic poem.

THE GRAIL SEARCH

At the time the Grail romances were being written in the twelfth and thirteenth centuries, anyone in Europe who practiced a religion or followed a spiritual path that differed from orthodox Christianity was likely to be burned at the stake. The first of these romances was written by Chrétien de Troyes, a relative of Hughes de Payen, the second by Wolfram von Essenbach, who was reputed to be a Templar. The sagas tell of a long and arduous quest to find a cup that is believed to be capable of returning the dead to life and healing the sick. In fact, the sagas can be interpreted as giving a very different message, for encoded within the story is a heretical guide to the spiritual pathway that can lead to enlightenment: the true teachings of Jesus.

The stories are a clever mix of pagan legend, Celtic folklore, Jewish mystical symbolism, alchemical and Cabbalistic ideas, and the traditions of the Rex Deus families, all overlaid by the mainstream Christian veneration for holy relics. The Grail itself has been described as a chalice, a cup, a stone that fell from heaven, a stone within a cup, and a magical bowl. The most widespread description of the Holy Grail is as the cup used by Joseph of Arimathea to catch the blood of Jesus at the Crucifixion, a story that has caught the imagination of Christians for the last two millennia, but one which was confected by someone with no knowledge of Jewish burial customs of the time. Handling corpses was women's work, and any man who did so had to be a close relative of the deceased who then had to undergo ritual purification for a week—hardly something that was likely to happen on the eve one of the most important religious festivals in the Jewish calendar, namely Passover. Orthodox Jewish burial tradition of that era also insists that to ensure life in the hereafter the body be interred in its entirety, a practice that the Hassidim, pious Jews, still follow to this day.

The immense popularity of the original Grail sagas posed a huge problem for the Catholic Church. Suppression was out of the question, because the stories had fired the imagination of the public. So, to counter these heretical tales, the Church confected its own version, a highly sanitized variation on the original theme that became known as the Vulgate Cycle, which later became inextricably mixed with the Arthurian legends.

RIGHT: A CHALICE REPRESENTING THE HOLY GRAIL. IN CHRISTIAN TRADITION, THE GRAIL WAS THE VESSEL USED BY JESUS AT THE LAST SUPPER AND BELIEVED TO POSSESS MIRACULOUS HEALING POWERS.

RIGHT: THE GRAIL ROMANCES SUGGEST THAT KING ARTHUR AND HIS KNIGHTS, DEPICTED HERE EMBARKING FOR THE HOLY LAND, TOOK PART IN THE CRUSADES.

hidden symbolism of the order

MUCH OF THE BELIEF SYSTEM OF THE REX DEUS INITIATES OF THE TEMPLAR ORDER WAS SECRETLY ENCODED IN SYMBOLIC FORM IN THE GREAT GOTHIC CATHEDRALS OF CHARTRES AND AMIENS AS WELL AS MANY CHURCHES IN THE TEMPLAR LANDS IN PROVENCE. IT CAN ALSO BE FOUND IN ROSSLYN CHAPEL IN SCOTLAND.

Three of the greatest memorials to the beliefs of the Knights Templar are the cathedrals of Chartres and Amiens in France and Rosslyn Chapel in Scotland. The first two were largely financed and constructed under the direct influence of the Templars. The third is far too late to be classed as a Templar building, although in many respects it was built—by Earl William St. Clair, who was described as '"one of the illuminati" (a term used to describe someone who had achieved spiritual enlightenment)—to commemorate Templar belief.

The scriptural validity of the Rex Deus line of transmission of spiritual teaching is commemorated by the carvings of the major Old Testament prophets that are to be found in the north portal of Chartres Cathedral, "the Portal of the Initiates." These give both explicit and coded references to the spiritual teaching that was passed down through the generations from ancient Egypt through the prophets of biblical Israel and indicate, unequivocally, that Jesus was an integral part of this line of transmission.

On the left side is a carving of Melchizedek, the priest-king of the Egyptian city of Salem, who carries the stone within a cup of the Grail sagas. Melchizedek paid homage to Abraham, who stands next to him with his son Isaac. The statues of Abraham and Isaac are a vivid reminder that human sacrifice was forbidden by God for all time, a concept that became an integral part of Jewish teaching. This also naturally applied to Jesus, who was a rabbi and devout Jew, and further reinforces the point that he came to reveal an ancient and revered spiritual path and not to redeem mankind from its sins as some form of vicarious human sacrifice, an idea that was completely unacceptable to the Jewish people. Next to Abraham we find Moses holding the tablets of the Law. He is bearing the serpent-entwined staff of office of the pharaohs to indicate his royal descent.

ABOVE: JOHN THE BAPTIST HOLDING THE AGNUS DEI, AND WITH A DRAGON BENEATH HIS FEET. THIS SYMBOLIZES HIS ROLE AS A MORTAL LINK BETWEEN SACRED KNOWLEDGE AND JESUS.

Beside Moses is his brother Aaron, another member of Egyptian royalty and an initiate into the Temple mysteries. He was the ancestor of the Cohens, the 24 hereditary high priests of the Temple of Jerusalem. The final figure in this tableau is King David, the father of Solomon, who was the builder of the temple from which the Templar Order took its name. Jesus, of course, was described as a direct descendant of the House of David. This row of carvings reflect the tradition of hereditary transmission that are described in *Custodians of Truth* by Tim Wallace-Murphy and

LEFT: A BAS-RELIEF SCULPTURE DEPICTING JESUS ABOVE THE TRIPLE DOORWAY ON THE WEST FRONT OF CHARTRES CATHEDRAL. HE IS BAREFOOT, HIS RIGHT HAND IS RAISED IN BLESSING AND HIS LEFT HAND HOLDS A BIBLE. HIS HEAD IS SURROUNDED BY A HALO CONTAINING A TEMPLAR CROSS, LA CROIX CÉLESTE OR THE CROSS OF UNIVERSAL KNOWLEDGE.

I, and show how the hidden wisdom of ancient Egypt was transmitted through the prophets of biblical Israel.

To the right of the portal stands a statue of John the Baptist carrying the Agnus Dei, the Lamb of God which represents Jesus. John's bare feet rest on a dragon, which, in Church symbolism, symbolizes the conquest of evil. However, in esoteric terms this image indicates that John became the human bridge between sacred knowledge, symbolized by the dragon, and Jesus, represented by the Lamb of God. Next to John stands Peter, who is clothed in a pectoral symbolic of the hereditary priesthood, encrusted with twelve stones. Beside Peter there is a carving of the prophet Elijah passing his cloak to his spiritual successor, Elisha, yet another sculpture validating the principle of spiritual transmission. At Chartres there are many other indications of Rex Deus involvement. Carvings of La Croix Fleury, an equal-armed cross with each arm surmounted with a stylized representation of the fleur-de-lis, can be found near the bases of the pillars supporting the canopy above the Portal of the Initiates. These have been there since the thirteenth century—the time of the building's original construction—and, although rare in this era, they always appear at sites that were under the patronage of one of the Rex Deus families.

THE CRUCIFIXION

Most Templar churches display no representation of the Crucifixion. Chartres Cathedral, still a major center of Christian worship, as it has been since its construction, has no carving that makes any reference to the Crucifixion dating from the first 200 years of its existence. The west front of Fulbertus' cathedral was incorporated into the present building and this contains an early stained-glass window that survived the fire which carries one depiction of the Crucifixion.

Just above the lintel of the three main doors in the west front is a narrow frieze that shows 38 scenes from Jesus' life, carved in fine detail, but with the Crucifixion conspicuous by its absence. This deliberate omission of any reference to the principal tenet of Christian belief and dogma is a reflection of the Templar inner-circle view that Jesus came to reveal and not to redeem. Among the Nag Hammadi scrolls of the Coptic Christians, discovered in Egypt in 1945, is the Gospel of Thomas, in which Jesus' initiatory teaching is evident. He is quoted as saying, "He who will drink from my mouth will become like me. I myself shall become he, and things that are hidden will be revealed to him," indicating that anyone following in Jesus' path will be led to enlightenment.

The Cathedral of Amiens was built, among other reasons, to house the reliquary allegedly containing the head of John the Baptist. However, it is also a sublime architectural and symbolic representation of the Gnostic principle of divine wisdom. Indeed, the French mystical writer François Cali claims that in traveling from the Cathedral of Chartres to that of Amiens, one makes an almost imperceptible transition "from the Love of God to the Love of Wisdom," and it is divine wisdom, or gnosis, to which he refers. The principle of gnosis is stressed by the most famous statue at Amiens, the carving of Jesus on the west front of the cathedral known as "the Beau Dieu." In this sculpture, Jesus is depicted standing on both a lion and a dragon, with the dragon representing not evil as the Church would claim but sacred knowledge. The themes of Gnostic teaching so central to the Rex Deus traditions of initiatory spirituality are repeated symbolically yet again in the plethora of quatrefoils on the west fronts of both

A DETAIL OF THE WEST FACADE OF THE CATHEDRAL OF NOTRE-DAME, AMIENS, WITH THE FAMOUS "BEAU DIEU" STATUE OF JESUS AT THE CENTER. MORE ELABORATE AND WITH MORE SCULPTURAL DECORATION THAN CHARTRES, AMIENS IS FULL OF SYMBOLISM.

Amiens Cathedral and Notre-Dame de Paris, which clearly depict alchymical symbolism. Alchemy was not, as it was popularly believed to be, a search for a magical elixir that would transmute base metals, such as lead, into gold. It was, like the Grail sagas, an allegorical description of the spiritual process of initiation which transmutes the "base metal" of earthly humanity into the "pure gold" of spiritual enlightenment. The theme of enlightenment crops up again in the architecture of Amiens Cathedral. Deliberately designed to enhance the healing power of light, the cathedral celebrates, perhaps by coincidence, the ultimate fulfillment of the spiritual path, the passage from darkness into the light of divine gnosis. All initiatory systems, irrespective of the culture or era in which they arise, are universally described as pathways from darkness into light.

The saint revered above all others at the Cathedral of Amiens is, of course, the teacher of Jesus, John the Baptist.

JOHN THE EVANGELIST

In churches associated with the Templars or the Rex Deus tradition, it would appear that two figures often appear to take precedence over Jesus. The first is his teacher and spiritual guide, John the Baptist; the second is John the Evangelist or John the Divine, sometimes described as "the disciple whom Jesus loved." John wrote many scriptural documents that have either been lost or suppressed by the Church, such as the Acts of John and the Gospel of Love. We do, however, still have the sublime initiatory document known as The Revelation of St. John that forms the final book in the New Testament canon.

The figure of John the Evangelist is less evident than John the Baptist and hovers in the background, highly influential but almost unseen. According to the nineteenth-century Pope Pius IX, the Templars "were followers of the Johannite heresy from the very beginning," yet the exact nature of the Johannite heresy has never been clearly defined. It has been

suggested that it pertained to the Templars' veneration of John the Baptist, but this was well-known at the time and accepted by the Church, even in that repressive era. The apprehension felt by the Church most probably arose from the Templars' secret adherence to the true teachings of Jesus, as recorded by John the Evangelist in the Gospel of Love, an initiatory document that survives in part, at least, in the Gospel according to St. John.

THE CULT OF THE BLACK MADONNA

The true origins of the Catholic cult of Mariolatry can be found in the pagan worship of a variety of divine mother figures. Mariolatry spread from Chartres throughout France, Spain, and much of Europe in the twelfth century, and was closely followed by veneration of the Black Madonna, yet there are some Black Madonna sites that predate this period. The Templars used their veneration of the Black Virgin to disguise their heretical worship of Isis and the Horus child, and the principle of divine wisdom. Thus, it is no surprise to discover that the peak years of growth of the worship of the Black Madonna coincided with the Templar era.

Disguised within this cult was Templar veneration of Mary Magdalene, who they believed was the wife of Jesus and the mother of his children. Devotion to the Magdalene was widespread both among the members of the order and throughout the lands it controlled. The English author Ean Begg identified 50 sites dedicated to Mary Magdalene that contain shrines of the Black Madonna. Mary Magdalene was given special status by the early Christian Gnostics because they believed that she was Jesus' favorite disciple,

THE VIRGIN OF THE PILLAR, ONE OF THE THREE INITIATORY BLACK MADONNAS FOUND IN CHARTRES CATHEDRAL. VENERATION OF THE BLACK MADONNA CAN BE TRACED BACK TO THE CULT OF MARIOLATRY AND THE ANCIENT WORSHIP OF DIVINE MOTHER FIGURES.

BLACK MADONNAS IN CHARTRES

THERE ARE THREE BLACK MADONNAS IN CHARTRES CATHEDRAL. THE FIRST IS IN THE CRYPT, NOTRE-DAME-SOUS-TERRE. ACCORDING TO THE OFFICIAL GUIDE, THE CRYPT WAS USED AS AN INITIATION CHAMBER. THE SECOND IS IN THE MAIN CATHEDRAL, THE VIRGIN OF THE PILLAR, DRESSED ACCORDING TO TRADITION IN HEAVY, ORNATE ROBES ARRANGED IN THE SHAPE OF A TRIANGLE. THE THIRD REPRESENTATION, NOTRE-DAME DE LA BELLE VERRIERE, IS FOUND IN A STAINED-GLASS WINDOW THAT SURVIVED THE TWELFTH-CENTURY FIRE.

and as such had been granted the highest level of gnosis. The European esoteric tradition describes Magdalene as "the symbol of divine wisdom." In the Nazarene tradition, she is often shown dressed in black like Isis; symbolically, in the Egyptian tradition, the color black indicates wisdom. She wears Sophia's crown of stars, while her infant wears the golden crown of royalty. Isis is the black Egyptian goddess, venerated as the initiate of light or enlightenment, the divine mother of the god Horus, embodying the Classical Greek goddess of wisdom, Sophia. Initiatory ceremonies and mystery rites were part of the original Egyptian cult of Isis, but we have no valid information on the nature of these rites as they were secret and not committed to writing.

The French historian Charles Bigarne, who has studied the cult, states that some statues of Isis bear the same inscription as that of the virgin found in the crypt at Chartres, Notre-Dame-Sous-Terre, the virgin about to give birth.

According to the twentieth-century initiate Rudolph Steiner, sacred symbolism can be interpreted at up to nine levels, depending on the degree of initiation of the viewer. The Black Madonna is a classic example of this, for at the simplest level she represents Mary, the mother of Jesus, with her child: in esoteric terms, the Black Madonna can also be interpreted as Mary Magdalene holding the child of Jesus; at another level she represents the seat of wisdom; and at another, Isis and the Horus child.

In pagan terms the Black Virgin symbolized the earth mother or the Egyptian goddess Anna, who again was represented as black. Was this a pagan precursor to the later Christian iconography of St. Anne, who occupies the central position in the stained-glass window above the Portal of the Initiates at Chartres Cathedral? St. Anne is shown with a black face, standing on a shield emblazoned with the insignia of the royal house of France, the fleur-de-lis, and

wearing a halo that is usually associated with the Magdalene. The Capetian kings, who adopted the fleur-de-lis as their emblem, ruled France for over nine centuries and claimed descent from Mary Magdalene. The earliest use of the fleur-de-lis to represent dynastic descent can be found carved near the top of a pillar erected by the Pharaoh Tuthmosis IV at the temple at Karnak in Egypt.

Another tradition attributing Egyptian origins to the Black Madonna can be found in the cult of the Magdalene at Orléans, where we find the virgin referred to as Mary the Egyptian, who traveled to Jerusalem from Alexandria, and is described as being "blackened by the heat and sun." She was a penitent sinner who allegedly withdrew to the desert for 47 years. There is a similar long-standing tradition that Mary Magdalene retired to a cave at St. Baume, near Aix-en-Provence, where she spent many years of her life in meditation and prayer.

Ean Begg, who has spent many years studying the cult of the Black Madonna and esoteric streams of spirituality in Christian Europe, claimed many years ago that the study of the history and legends of the Black Virgin may yet reveal a heretical sect with the power to shock and astonish even current post-Christian attitudes, and a secret involving political forces still influential today. He wrote this several years before Tim Wallace-Murphy and I first brought the Rex Deus tradition into the public domain.

You might have expected Bernard of Clairvaux, as the leading churchman of his time, simply to follow the Christian dogma of his time, yet he preached 120 sermons on the *Song of Songs*, an initiatory source that was traditionally associated with the Magdalene. The cult of the Black Madonna and the Magdalene are explicitly linked when the female lover says, "I am black but comely." Cult figures of importance to the Templars and their spiritual heirs, the Freemasons, are not restricted to the Magdalene or the two St. Johns, for another

LEFT: THE STAINED-GLASS WINDOW
AT ROSSLYN CHAPEL IN SCOTLAND,
ERECTED BY THE FREEMASONS
SHOWING ST. GEORGE STANDING ON
A ROSE-COLORED BOARD DECORATED
WITH ROSETTES, A SYMBOLIC
REFERENCE TO THE BABYLONIAN
GODDESS ISHTAR.

FAR LEFT: THE TRADITION OF THE
BLACK MADONNA IS OFTEN
ASSOCIATED WITH THE ANCIENT
EGYPTIAN GODDESS ISIS,
WHO WAS VENERATED BY
THE TEMPLARS.

enigmatic figure in both traditions is that of St. George, who later became the patron saint of England.

ST. GEORGE

The figure of St. George is of particular interest. He was reputed to be an Armenian, who the fifth-century pope, Gelasius, described as a "saint, venerated by man, but whose acts were known only to God." The earliest known religious character on whom St. George is based is the god Tammuz, known as the Lord of Life and Death. In Babylonian mythology he is described as the son, spouse, or brother of the goddess Ishtar. In Rosslyn Chapel in Scotland there is an unusual stained-glass window depicting St. George standing on a rose-colored board decorated with roses or rosettes that are a symbolic link to the goddess Ishtar and in turn to Tammuz. The reason that the patron saint of England is being celebrated in a Scottish chapel is that Rosslyn was built as a memorial to the Templars, so it is perfectly natural that one of the figures venerated by them should be found there. This commemoration also provides a clue to links between the Templars and the Sufis, who were supposedly sworn enemies, for there is growing acceptance for the idea that St. George, Tammuz, and El Khidir are the same person portrayed in different mythological guises. El Khidir is the legendary mystical teacher of the Sufis and is known by the title of the "green" or "verdant one." Green, symbolic of initiation, also signified his legendary status as both an initiate and the supreme teacher of the spiritual mysteries.

In France the papal commissioners were presented with the brothers' daily prayers, which included prayers to Mary, the Star of the Sea, Jesus, John the Evangelist, and St. George. Here, the heretical appears again in the guise of orthodox Christianity, although it is doubtful that the ordinary brothers, or the papal commissioners, knew that

there was any heretical content to their prayers, for they had no knowledge of the high level of initiation into the spiritual mysteries attained by these four figures.

THE VIRGIN MARY

The Templars of the inner circle in particular venerated Mary Magdalene, following the instructions of Bernard of Clairvaux when he enjoined them to make, "Obedience to Bethany and the House of Mary and Martha"—in other words, obedience and loyalty to the dynasty founded by Mary Magdalene and Jesus. However, the ordinary brothers followed the Catholic Church in their veneration of Mary, the mother of Jesus. Many of the donation charters included Mary in their title, and outwardly she was the patron saint of the order. Mary, the mother of Jesus, was brought up and educated at the Temple school for girls in Jerusalem. She was visited by the priest known by the title of "the Gabriel," an event that has been preserved in Christian

teaching as the visit by the archangel Gabriel to inform her of the immaculate conception of Jesus. According to an ancient legend that is preserved in *Legenda Aurea of Jacobus de Voragine* (1267), Mary was brought up in the Temple, thus reinforcing the tradition of Rex Deus. It has been claimed that the heretical veneration of Mary Magdalene and the child she bore Jesus is often disguised within the adoration of the Madonna and Child, or Mary and Jesus. In recent years more credence has been given to the suggestion that many of the great Notre-Dame cathedrals in northern Europe were dedicated not to Mary, the mother of Jesus, but to Mary Magdalene, his wife.

LEFT: A CARVING OF THE MADONNA AND CHILD ON THE WEST FRONT OF THE CATHEDRAL OF NOTRE-DAME DE PARIS. MARY IS ENTHRONED IN GLORY, CROWNED AS THE QUEEN OF HEAVEN; JESUS SEATED ON HER LAP HAS HIS RIGHT HAND RAISED IN BLESSING.

ABOVE: A DEPICTION OF TWO BROTHERS ON ONE HORSE, ONE OF THE SIGNS OF TEMPLAR ATTRIBUTION AND A SYMBOL THAT WAS USED ON MANY TEMPLAR SEALS, REPRESENTING COMMUNAL POVERTY AND FRATERNITY.

ROSSLYN CHAPEL

Rosslyn Chapel lies approximately seven miles to the south of Edinburgh in Scotland, in the village of Roslin. It was constructed in the second half of the fifteenth century by the Baron of Roslin, William St. Clair, Earl of Orkney, the leading member of one of the Rex Deus families at that time, whose family had been heavily involved with the Templar Order. The chapel was built far too late to be classed as a Templar church, but it is nonetheless heavily imbued with Templar symbolism.

Rosslyn Chapel contains all six of the symbols that determine a Templar building as set down by Durbec, the

French Templar scholar: the two brothers on one horse, the Veil of Veronica or Mandylion, the Agnus Dei, the floriated cross, the five-pointed star, and the dove with the olive branch in its beak. The two brothers on one horse are disguised as a carving of Ladislaus Leslyn and Princess Margaret; the Mandylion is in plain view, decorating the top of a pillar, as is the Agnus Dei. The floriated cross is found on a grave marker of an earlier St. Clair, which was brought into the chapel some ten years ago. The five-pointed star and dove are hidden high up in the roof on the north side, where we also find rosettes similar to those decorating the checker-board on which St. George stands in the stained-glass window. The windows were added in Victorian times yet they embody much of the symbolism that is associated with Rex Deus and the Order of the Knights Templar.

Earl William was aware that books and people could be burned, so he encoded the ancient knowledge handed down through the generations in the carvings in the chapel. There are also many symbolic representations of other spiritual pathways unknown in the West at the time, that could only have come to Earl William through the oral traditions of Rex Deus. Where else could William St. Clair obtain this knowledge? One possible answer is from the scrolls discovered by the first Templars under the Temple Mount, which may have been taken to Roslin for safekeeping by the St. Clairs. Even the name Roslin itself echoes the all-pervading theme of secrecy, for it translates as "ancient knowledge passed down the generations." The chapel was built in an era when ancient and heretical knowledge had to remain secret if you wished to avoid being tried for heresy and executed, so Earl William hedged

his bets and included one tiny representation of the
Crucifixion, measuring all of four inches square, tucked away
almost unnoticed on top of a small pillar by the north door.

In the context of the Knights Templar, ancient knowledge
implies some degree of access to its fruits: spiritual insight,
political power, and wealth. If the Templars entrusted the St.
Clair family with secret knowledge, then it is highly probable
that, as French Masonic tradition recounts, they would also
have been chosen to be the guardians of some if not all of
the vanished Templar treasure.

LEFT: ROSSLYN CHAPEL FROM
THE NORTHWEST, SHOWING
THE FLYING BUTTRESSES,
PINNACLES, AND BARREL-VAULTED
STONE ROOF. THE BAPTISTERY
WHICH PROJECTS FROM THE
INCOMPLETE TRANSEPT WALL IS
A RECENT VICTORIAN ADDITION.

ABOVE AND RIGHT: NUMEROUS
CARVINGS INSIDE ROSSLYN CHAPEL
CARRY MANY TEMPLAR
REFERENCES. ABOVE IS THE AGNUS
DEI CARVING AND RIGHT IS THE
APPRENTICE PILLAR.

decline and fall

THE SECOND HALF OF THE THIRTEENTH CENTURY BROUGHT THE LOSS OF MUCH TERRITORY IN THE EAST, WITH JERUSALEM REGAINED BRIEFLY BY TREATY, ONLY TO BE LOST FOREVER. THE FALL OF ACRE SAW THE FINAL EXPULSION OF THE CRUSADERS FROM THE HOLY LAND.

After the capture of Jerusalem in 1187, the remaining crusader states in the Holy Land were whittled away piecemeal until, in 1291, Christian forces lost their final footholds in the East with the fall of Acre, Beirut, and Sidon. Thus the Templar Order lost the principal reason for its existence. The reasons behind these events were complex, for wars and conflict in Europe had distracted attention from the Holy Land, significantly reducing support for the crusaders' cause. The papacy was at war with Frederick II of Germany, and during the 1260s, European crusaders were diverted to fight in Sicily. Meanwhile, King Henry III of England was squabbling with his barons, a situation that lasted until 1267; Italian communes were at war with each other; and the Mongols conquered much of Central Asia and invaded Mesopotamia and Eastern Europe, as a result of which the trade routes moved northward. The remnants of the crusader states were thus further impoverished, for trade that had been a vital source of income for the crusader states was now diverted to Venice, Pisa, and Genoa. By 1291, England and France were on the verge of war as, in the Holy Land, one crusader castle after another fell into enemy hands.

These were the main contributory factors that led to the irreversible decline of European power in the Holy Land. However, what finally sealed the fate of the crusader states was the unification of the Muslims under the Mamluks, who turned their armies into an efficient military body that overcame the resistance of the weakened crusader forces. A series of short-term truces were agreed but, fundamentally, the sultan was prepared to use any pretext to destroy the hated Christian invaders.

THE FIFTH CRUSADE

In 1199, Pope Innocent III complained that no one except him seemed interested in pursuing another crusade. To their eternal credit, the Templars played no part whatsoever in the ill-conceived Fourth Crusade (1201–1204), which was a disaster before it even started. The crusaders besieged and sacked the Christian city of Constantinople and never reached the Holy Land at all. Pope Innocent died in 1216, and his successor Honorius III continued with the plans for a new crusade, the fifth, which eventually materialized in 1218. On this occasion, however, the Templar Order did play a significant role.

Indeed, Pope Honorius issued instructions to the Grand Masters of the Templars and Hospitallers to meet the leaders of the crusade, King Andrew of Hungary and Duke Leopold of Austria, in Cyprus. The two leaders arrived separately with their armies in the East and made plans to attack Damascus. These were shelved in favor of mounting an attack on the key city of Damietta in Egypt. Led by the king of Jerusalem, the crusaders, reinforced by the Templars, landed at Damietta in June 1218.

The Templars rapidly adapted their methods to cope with fighting in the waterlogged Nile delta. They used a fleet of ships and pontoons, and swiftly developed the ability to deal with the difficulties inherent in campaigning in swamps, thus proving their capability as soldiers and engineers of genius, for this sort of warfare differed greatly from that fought on the sunbaked hills of Palestine. The Egyptian city was quickly taken, and the sultan offered Jerusalem back to the crusaders if only they would return the city of Damietta to his control. The papal legate, Pelagius, refused. For, unless the lands surrounding Jerusalem were also ceded to the crusaders it would be impossible to hold onto the Holy City, an almost identical situation to that which had arisen during the Third Crusade. A decision was made to await the arrival of Emperor Frederick II from Germany before taking any further action, but the imperial army failed to arrive. Pelagius ordered the crusading army to advance up the Nile, against the advice of the Templars, who believed that their resources were already overstretched. When the crusaders reached the town of Mansurah, the Muslim army trapped them by cutting off their retreat and halting their advance by opening the sluice gates on the river, flooding the crusaders into submission. A truce that was to last for eight years was agreed, and Damietta was surrendered.

THE BATTLE OF DAMIETTA IN THE NILE DELTA IN EGYPT THAT TOOK PLACE IN 1221 DURING THE FIFTH CRUSADE. IT ENDED WHEN THE CRUSADERS SURRENDERED TO THE EGYPTIAN FORCES AFTER AGREEING TO A TRUCE THAT WAS TO LAST FOR EIGHT YEARS.

MAJOR CRUSADES IN THE 13TH CENTURY

1201–1204	THE FOURTH CRUSADE. CONSTANTINOPLE CAPTURED.
1217–1221	THE FIFTH CRUSADE IN WHICH EGYPT WAS ATTACKED.
1228–1229	THE CRUSADE OF EMPEROR FREDERICK II OF GERMANY DURING WHICH JERUSALEM WAS RECOVERED BY TREATY.
1249–1254	THE FIRST CRUSADE OF KING LOUIS IX OF FRANCE TO EGYPT.
1270	THE SECOND CRUSADE OF KING LOUIS.
1291	ACRE IS CAPTURED BY MUSLIM FORCES, MARKING THE END OF THE CRUSADES IN THE HOLY LAND. REMAINING CHRISTIAN TERRITORIES FALL SOON AFTER.

THE HOLY ROMAN EMPEROR, FREDERICK II

At his coronation in 1212, the Holy Roman Emperor Frederick II had publicly vowed to take the Cross and go on crusade. The grandson of Frederick Barbarossa and a legitimate claimant to the throne of Jerusalem through his wife, Constance of Aragon, he had succeeded to the throne of Germany at the age of three. He spoke fluent Italian, French, German, Greek, Latin, and Arabic, and had been brought up on the island of Sicily where he was exposed to Arab culture.

Frederick and some of his army eventually reached Acre in September 1228, after a difficult passage. Many of his forces fell ill, necessitating an enforced delay at Otranto. This enraged Pope Gregory IX, who immediately excommunicated the emperor. When Frederick arrived once more at Acre the following spring, he was excommunicated again. The second time was for defying the pope and continuing the crusade while excommunicated. This situation hardly concerned him, for Frederick was not driven so much by religious fervor as by personal ambition, and he believed that success in the Holy Land would give him power over the papacy. However, by the time he finally reached Acre news of his excommunication had spread and he was barred from leading the crusade. In this dispute, the Templars and Hospitallers sided with the pope while the Teutonic Knights supported the emperor.

JERUSALEM REGAINED

Frederick's wife died in childbirth and, thereby, he lost his claim to the throne of Jerusalem, except as regent for his infant son, Conrad. Having also lost his position as leader of the crusade he marched to 'Atlit and demanded that the Templars hand over the castle to him to be garrisoned by his forces. The Templars refused, and he returned to Acre from where he marched on Jaffa. Having refused to serve under the emperor, the Templars and Hospitallers followed a day behind. It was only when Frederick handed command over to his generals that the two principal military orders rejoined the crusaders. While the Templars were always prepared to fight, Frederick preferred to use negotiation and in a coup previously thought impossible he regained possession of the Holy City by agreeing a ten-year truce with the Egyptian sultan during which Jerusalem was returned to Christian control, but leaving the Muslims with absolute authority over the Temple Mount.

Frederick crowned himself king of Jerusalem in March 1229, supported only by the Teutonic knights. The Templars and Hospitallers were conspicuous by their absence, for the animosity that existed between the Knights Templar and the emperor fueled rumors that claimed that each side had plans to assassinate the leaders of their opponents. Indeed, at one point Frederick tried to take the Templar compound in Acre by force but failed. The very public consequences of Frederick's high-handed actions became vividly apparent when, on leaving the Holy Land on May 1, 1229, his departure was celebrated by jeering crowds who pelted him with dung. Two years later, in 1231, Frederick's representative, Filangieri, made Acre the objective of another attack. Like his master, Filangieri also failed to take the city but managed to set up a base at Tyre. There was now a civil war going on in the Holy Land between the crusaders and Frederick's forces. The antagonism continued until just prior to the ending of the ten-year truce with the sultan.

POLITICAL AMBITION AND THE DESIRE FOR POWER OVER THE PAPACY COMPELLED FREDERICK II TO EMBARK ON A SERIES OF CRUSADES. IN 1229, HE BECAME KING OF JERUSALEM.

A year later, Duke Richard of Cornwall, the brother-in-law of King Henry III of England, arrived with a crusading army. His first tasks were to free the Christian captives held in Damascus and Cairo and to obtain recognition for the lands recently ceded to the crusaders. As soon as Richard returned to England the Templars attacked the city of Hebron and retook Nablus. Once again the Templars found themselves embroiled in conflict with both the imperial forces and the Hospitallers, who had been opposed to their attacks on Hebron and Nablus. At this juncture, Filangieri set his sights on Acre yet again and this time used the Hospitallers' compound as a base from which to launch his attack. The Templars retaliated and besieged the Hospitallers' headquarters for the next six months.

JERUSALEM LOST FOREVER

A fresh crisis arose in 1244, when war broke out once more between Egypt and Damascus. Reinforced by the Khorezmanian Turks, a fierce tribe of mercenary nomads, Egyptian forces swept south from Edessa and attacked Jerusalem, which fell a month later. The Holy City was lost to the Christians yet again, but this time permanently. The bones of Godfroi de Bouillon and other kings of Jerusalem were disinterred from the Church of the Holy Sepulchre, and then the church was set alight.

The Egyptian and Turkish armies joined forces at Gaza, and this army was attacked by Christian forces at La Forbie. It was an unmitigated disaster, for the Damascan troops promptly deserted their Christian allies and fled the field, leaving the Christian forces to be slaughtered by the Muslims. Some 800 crusaders were taken prisoner and sold into slavery, among them the Grand Master of the Templars. Thirty-three Templar knights survived, but they had lost between 260 and 300 of their comrades in the battle. Damascus fell to the Egyptians the following year.

SAINT LOUIS

In 1248, King Louis IX of France set sail from Aigues-Mort in the Camargue on his first crusade to the Holy Land, and, after over-wintering in Cyprus, landed in Egypt in June 1249. His forces recaptured Damietta and then marched

THE CRUSADES THAT FAILED

Yet another crusade was called in 1239, by Pope Gregory, but only Count Theobold of Champagne took up the cross. The sultan of Egypt had died the year before, and anarchy was rife in the Muslim world as a number of claimants fought for the title. So when Theobald arrived in the East he found that the Templars had encouraged the barons to make an alliance with the ruler of Damascus, who had agreed to allow the Christians to retake control of lands that had been seized by the Muslims in return for support in his fight against the Egyptians. Part of Theobold's army commanded by Henry, Count of Bar, was decisively defeated at Gaza by Egyptian forces. The blame for this defeat fell on the shoulders of the Templars and Hospitallers who, having assessed the inherent danger of attacking a far superior force, had refused to support Henry in his attack.

AN ILLUSTRATION OF KING LOUIS IX OF
FRANCE, KNOWN AS ST. LOUIS, EMBARKING
FROM AIGUES-MORT IN THE RHONE DELTA,
FRANCE, EN ROUTE FOR THE CRUSADES.

south toward Cairo, with the Templars forming the vanguard. The army wasted months trying to cross a branch of the River Nile without success. When they eventually found a ford, a column that included Templars headed the crossing, but events took a disastrous turn for the worse. Louis's brother Richard decided not to wait until all of the crusading forces had crossed the river and attacked the Muslims with those he had at his disposal, driving the enemy back to the town of Mansurah. Unfortunately the knight holding the bridle of Richard's horse was deaf and failed to impart a message from the Templars to the effect that they were angry with Richard for his foolhardy action. Richard ordered the Christian forces to pursue the Muslim army, and the Templars, afraid of losing face, had no choice but to follow. The crusaders then found themselves trapped in the narrow streets of Mansurah by wooden beams and other debris that had been used to build blockades. In the chaos that followed 280 Templars and 300 secular knights lost their lives. Richard foolishly tried to swim to safety in full armor and drowned; the Templar Grand Master Guillaume de Sonnac lost an eye, dying from further wounds three days later when the army made a second onslaught on the town. Mansurah was not going to be an easy prize.

The crusading army under Louis set siege to the city, but while they were entrenched outside the walls the Muslims cut off their supply lines from Damietta, leaving them without fresh food. Dysentery soon ravaged the camp, and Louis decided to open negotiations. He was unsuccessful, and after a seven-week siege the Christian forces began to withdraw. The Muslims harried their retreat and several thousand were killed; only three Templars survived. The Muslims then took almost the entire army captive, including King Louis. The king's ransom was the return of Damietta to the Muslims, while the ransom for the remainder of the captives was set at 500,000 livres.

The Muslims took control of Damietta and Louis was released. The ransom for the remaining captives was 30,000 livres short. Louis agreed that the Templars should be asked to supply the balance, but they at first refused on the grounds that the money belonged to those who had deposited it and could not be released without their permission. The Templar marshal suggested that there was nothing to stop the money being taken by force; in other words he was issuing a challenge to steal it so that he would not be forced to break his vow to protect it. However, he did eventually order it to be handed over.

Louis left the Holy Land in 1254, having spent nearly five years in the East. Although the crusade had failed miserably in Egypt it had succeeded in improving fortifications in some of the key cities, such as Sidon and Acre. Louis pledged to supply French troops to garrison them; the high cost of maintaining the castles that were further inland fell to the military orders. In the years Louis spent in the East he had injected more than 11 times the annual income of his kingdom in his support of the Holy Land, a total of 1.3 million livres tournois.

The remaining half of the thirteenth century lurched from one crisis to another. In the 1260s, the Templar castle of Safed and the Hospitallers castle, Krak des Chevaliers, fell. Antioch was lost in 1268, and the Templar possessions in the Amanus March were abandoned. A new crusade was called at the Council of Lyons but, although the Templars played a prominent role in the talks to start it, no agreement was forthcoming. Back in the Holy Land, factional disputes about who was the rightful claimant to the throne of Jerusalem were tearing the country apart, with the Templars supporting Charles of Anjou against King Hugh III of Jerusalem, who was incensed at the Templars' disregard for any law but their own. He left for Cyprus, losing the kingdom in the process. The Templars' involvement in the civil war that took place in the county of Tripoli led to their Grand Master, Guillaume de Beaujeu, being branded as untrustworthy, although he did negotiate a ten-year truce with the Mamluks that was subsequently broken in 1285.

THE FALL OF ACRE

In April 1291, Acre became the last major Christian stronghold in the Holy Land to come under attack, and was besieged for six weeks. The opposing sides fought in the streets, and

Guillaume de Beaujeu died in action, having foolishly rushed out to help repel the Mamluks without putting on all of his armor. His death sealed the fate of the last bastion of the kingdom of Jerusalem, for within hours the city was overrun. The military orders helped with the evacuation of the Christians, and those inhabitants who could escape sought ships in the port and fled to Cyprus. The Templar commander set sail with the Templar treasure aboard his ship.

A contemporary report states that 7,000 people fled to the Templar house in the city, which was located in a strong defensive position overlooking the sea, and surrounded by "good walls" that were 28 feet (8.5 meters) thick. They defended it for 12 days, whereupon they realized they had no supplies and no way of obtaining any. The Templars then "rushed out strenuously on the Saracens and strongly threw down many of their adversaries." The Templars were all slaughtered.

The fall of Acre was to prove to be a pivotal point, not only in terms of Christendom's hold on the Holy Land, but in particular for the Knights Templar. It is ironic that while the Templars were the last to give up the fight in Acre, they would eventually come to be blamed for the ultimate loss of the Holy Land.

The ignominious defeat effectively heralded the end of an era. Other ideals had captured the imagination and interest of the kings and nobility of Europe, and even strenuous papal efforts to raise further crusades to the Holy Land were to be met with little response. Accusations would eventually feed a growing contempt for the Templar Order, and would see their demise at the hands of a king determined to capitalize on their growing unpopularity for his own ends.

The cities of Tyre, Beirut, and Tortosa held out after the fall of Acre, but not for long, with Castle Pilgrim—which was the only stronghold never to have been taken thus far—the last to fall in August 1291. To prevent the Templars reoccupying the site should they ever return to the Holy Land, the Mamluks completely dismantled the fortress, stone by stone. The garrisons of these towns fell back to Cyprus, where they began negotiations for another crusade. One item that now rode high on the agenda of Pope Nicholas IV was the amalgamation of the military orders into one body.

LEFT: THE OUTER WALL AND DITCH OF THE CASTLE OF TORTOSA, WHICH WAS SUCCESSFULLY DEFENDED BY THE KNIGHTS TEMPLAR IN 1188, LED BY GERARD DE RIDEFORT—THE SARACEN ARMY RETREATED WITHOUT TAKING IT.

ABOVE: KOLOSSI CASTLE HAD BEEN BUILT BY THE CRUSADERS AT LIMASSOL, THE CAPITAL OF CYPRUS. CYPRUS WAS SOLD TO THE TEMPLARS BY RICHARD I OF ENGLAND, AND LATER BECAME THE HEADQUARTERS OF THE ORDER.

JACQUES DE MOLAY

Very little is known of Jacques de Molay's years as a member of the Templar Order until after he became the twenty-third Grand Master in 1292. Allegations of irregularities in the election were rife, indeed the Grand Master of the Hospitallers was invited to act as both an adviser and arbitrator. In the spring of 1293, Jacques de Molay left Cyprus. He landed in Marseilles where he began preparations for a general chapter meeting to be held in August of that year. Toward the end of the year he made a trip to England, where he remained until the early summer

of 1294, when he left for Aragon. From Aragon he journeyed to Rome, and stayed in the kingdom of Charles of Anjou. He then took possession of the Benedictine monastery of Torre Maggiore, which was given to the order by the papacy.

Jacques de Molay's visit to the West had two objectives. The first was to enlist support so that the order would be able to return to the Holy Land, and fulfil its traditional goals, with the recapture of Jerusalem as the first priority. His second objective was to reform the order and make it the driving force behind a new crusade to effect a reconquest, an event that failed to materialize, despite Pope Nicholas IV issuing several papal bulls calling for a new crusade. After these appeals failed, de Molay spent most of his time as head of the Templar Order on Cyprus, staying at the headquarters in Limassol in the south of the island until he was summoned to France by the pope.

ABOVE: AFTER THE FALL OF ACRE. POPE NICHOLAS IV (1288–92) CALLED FOR A NEW CRUSADE. HE CITED DISPUTES BETWEEN THE TEMPLARS AND HOSPITALLERS AS ONE OF THE REASONS FOR THE DEFEAT AND WANTED THE TWO ORDERS TO MERGE.

Deſsiné par Rogier

Gravé par Geille.

JACQUES DE MOLAY, THE LAST GRAND
MASTER OF THE TEMPLAR ORDER, WHOSE
ELECTION WAS DEEMED SOMEWHAT SUSPECT.

AFTER FAILING IN HIS ATTEMPTS TO REFORM
THE ORDER AND SECURE A NEW CRUSADE, HE
REMAINED IN CYPRUS UNTIL 1306.

the trial of the templars

WITH THE LOSS OF THE HOLY LAND, THE TEMPLARS LOST THEIR PRINCIPAL *RAISON D'ETRE*, AND THIS INCREDIBLY WEALTHY ORDER BECAME THE TARGET OF NAKED GREED. AIDED BY THE POPE, KING PHILIPPE IV OF FRANCE USED TRUMPED-UP CHARGES OF HERESY TO DESTROY THEM.

acques de Molay left the island of Cyprus in the fall of 1306, never to return. Pope Nicholas IV had summoned de Molay and Foulques de Villaret, the Grand Master of the Hospitallers, to France to discuss the plans for the crusade and the amalgamation of the orders. He instructed them to "travel as secretly as possible and with a very small train, as you will find plenty of your knights this side of the sea." De Villaret declined the invitation, as he was engaged in an assault on the Turkish stronghold of Rhodes, a situation that was public knowledge. Despite his reservations, Jacques de Molay accepted and set out for France, defying the instructions of the pope by sailing with a fleet of 18 ships, on board which were 60 of the order's senior knights, most of the "nucleus." He brought 150,000 florins and a large amount of silver bullion that needed 12 packhorses to carry it, which he intended to use as a bribe to prevent the proposed merger. As a matter of courtesy, the king welcomed him on his arrival at the Templar headquarters in Paris, and saw the treasure train entering the Temple.

Jacques de Molay had categorically rejected the idea of the unification of the two military orders in a memorandum he addressed to the pope in 1306. He claimed that, as the Brothers had been guided by God in their choice of which order they would join, it would amount to blasphemy if they were asked to change their allegiance. He also objected on the grounds that they were more effective as individual organizations, and that if they were joined it would lead to resentment, as many officials would no longer be needed and would lose their posts. And of course there was the matter of each order's individual property and wealth, which could create further conflict if the two became one. He would of course have been unable to disclose to either the king or the pope the fact that the Templars had been created by the descendants of the high priests of the original Temple of Jerusalem, who had their own agenda.

JACQUES DE MOLAY

JACQUES DE MOLAY WAS BORN IN 1244 IN VITREY, IN THE DEPARTMENT OF HAUTE SAONE IN FRANCE. HE JOINED THE TEMPLARS AT THE AGE OF 21 AND ROSE RAPIDLY THROUGH THE RANKS. HE WAS APPOINTED TO THE POSITION OF VISITOR GENERAL AND LATER HELD THE POST OF GRAND PRECEPTOR OF ALL ENGLAND BEFORE FINALLY BEING ELECTED AS THE LAST GRAND MASTER IN 1292. THE DAY BEFORE HIS ARREST IN 1307, HE HAD ACTED AS PALL BEARER AT THE FUNERAL OF KING PHILIPPE IV'S SISTER-IN-LAW. HE WAS BURNED AS A LAPSED HERETIC IN 1314.

The question of amalgamating the military orders had first been discussed at the Council of Lyons in 1274, but was dropped when it was pointed out that such a combined order would become far too powerful to control. However, the French government continued to press for the merger, although it stayed silent about what it thought should be done with them afterward. Contemporary writers claimed that the true aim was to place the new unified military order under the command of the sons of the king of France and, thereby, bring this powerful and immensely wealthy order under the direct control of Philippe IV.

PHILIPPE LE BEL

Known as Philippe le Bel, Philippe IV, grandson of Louis IX (canonized for his part in the crusades to the Holy Land), succeeded to the throne of France in October 1285. The kingdom of France had grown considerably, acquiring the provinces of Normandy, Anjou, Maine, Touraine, and, as a result of the Albigensian Crusade, the whole of the Languedoc. This debt-ridden kingdom's financial difficulties were exacerbated by the king's involvement in several wars. Philippe levied a ten percent tax on the Church and imposed a harsh tax on the Lombard and Florentine bankers of Italian origin whose business had spread across Europe. The Languedoc was subjected to punitive financial impositions, and he repeatedly debased the national coinage by reminting it with a lower precious-metal content. He also seized the property of the Jews and expelled them from France. His debt to the Lombard bankers exceeded 80,000 livres

RIGHT: THE PARIS TEMPLE, c. 1450.
HEADQUARTERS OF THE TEMPLAR
ORDER IN FRANCE WHICH HOUSED
THE CENTER FOR ADMINISTRATION
AND TREASURY. IT WAS NOT ONLY
THE REPOSITORY FOR TEMPLAR
MONEY BUT ALSO USED BY THE
KING OF FRANCE TO SAFEGUARD HIS
TAX REVENUE.

LEFT: ILLUSTRATION FROM TREATISE
OF THE VICES BY COCHARELLI OF
GENOA DEPICTING THE DESTRUCTION
OF THE TEMPLARS AND THE DEATH
OF PHILIP IV.

tournois, so he then imprisoned them and also seized
their assets, thus canceling his debt and producing
considerable income. Philippe connived and plotted to
ensure the election of a French candidate for the papacy,
Archbishop Bertrand de Gotte of Bordeaux, who took the
name of Pope Clement V in 1305. Philippe imposed
certain conditions in exchange for his support, including
the right to retain all tithes collected from the French
clergy for five years. Philippe also insisted that the new
pope reside in Avignon in France rather than in Rome,
thus placing him under the direct control and influence of
the king. To show his gratitude for Philippe's support,
Pope Clement almost immediately appointed 12 of the
king's associates as cardinals. A secret condition was
imposed by the king that was disclosed six months after
the papal coronation.

As a young man Philippe had applied to join the Templar Order but had been refused, which left him bitterly resentful. Civil unrest was rife in his nearly bankrupt kingdom, and during one riot he took refuge in the Paris Temple, where he was overawed by the enormous amount of bullion he saw there. He decided to appropriate the Templar treasure and get himself out of debt.

FRIDAY THE THIRTEENTH

At dawn on the morning of Friday, October 13, 1307, the royal seneschals of France opened the sealed orders they had received on September 14 instructing them to arrest the entire Templar brotherhood. The charge leveled at the order was described as "a bitter thing, a lamentable thing, a thing which is horrible to contemplate, terrible to hear of, a detestable crime, an execrable evil, an abominable work, a detestable disgrace, a thing almost inhuman, indeed set apart from all humanity." The Grand Master, 60 knights of the inner circle, and all but 24 of the knights residing in France were arrested. The arrests were made without warning, yet not all the Templars were apprehended; some escaped from La Rochelle with the fleet of 18 ships that had borne Jacques de Molay to France, taking the Temple treasure with them.

Philippe le Bel justified his actions by claiming that he had taken them at the behest of the Chief Inquisitor of France, Guillaume de Plaisians, who was not only deputy to the pope but also the king's personal confessor.

Philippe, an arrogant bully and a religious fanatic, was aided in his plotting by Guillaume de Nogaret, the Keeper of the Seals, who was even more zealous than the king. Despite the fact that Pope Clement was the king's puppet, he was outraged at Philippe's actions against the Templars, who, through the statutes laid down at their foundation, were answerable only to the pope. Clement wrote a letter to Philippe, stating that he had "violated every rule" by arresting the Templars, which Clement saw as an "act of contempt towards ourselves and the Roman Church." The crowned heads of Europe were horrified at Philippe's action; James II of Aragon was not the only one to believe that the charges brought against the order were fabricated so that Philippe, who everyone knew was insolvent, could take possession of the Templar treasure.

THE ACCUSATIONS

The Templars were arrested on charges of heresy, sodomy, and blasphemy. The Church historian David Christie-Murray defines heresy as, "An opinion held by a minority of men which the majority declares unacceptable and is powerful enough to punish." The Christian theologian St. Augustine, who became bishop of Hippo in 396 CE, defined it as, "The distortion of a revealed truth by a believer or an unbeliever," with the ambiguous term "revealed truth" defined, by the Church of course, as, "What the Church itself has declared to be revealed truth."

One charge levied against the Templars was that of causing Christ "injuries more terrible than those he endured on the cross." Specific accusations were considerable, and included denial of Jesus, defiling the Cross, adoration of an idol known as Baphomet, performing a perverted sacrament, wearing a cord of heretical significance, ritual murder, a ritual kiss, alteration in the ceremony of the Mass, an unorthodox form of absolution, immorality, and treachery to other sections of the Christian forces.

The charge of immorality was commonly used against anyone accused of heresy by the Inquisition. The charges of treachery, however, may have arisen from the Templars' strategic incompetence rather than actual betrayal of their fellow soldiers. As the Templar inner circle would have had no faith in the Pauline concept of redemption that arose as a result of Jesus' sacrifice at Golgotha, the charge of denying him and defiling the Cross may have had some degree of truth. The charges of perverting the sacrament and altering the Mass are highly questionable in view of the fact that the majority of Templars were staunch Catholics and only the inner circle of Templars believed that Jesus came to reveal not to redeem. The charge of wearing a cord of heretical significance could also be true, as the Templars used a cable-tow noose in their initiation ceremonies, as do the Freemasons today.

Although the arrests and accusations were sanctioned by the papal inquisitor, they did not follow the usual procedure whereby the arrest and custody of the heretics be made by a Church court, after which they were tried under Church law and released to the secular authority for punishment if found guilty. In this instance, the arrests were carried out under the direct authority of the king.

T.3669.

FAR LEFT: THE OFFICIAL RECORD OF THE PROCEEDINGS OF THE TRIAL OF THE TEMPLARS IN ENGLAND.

LEFT: A PAINTING DEPICTING THE FANATICAL PRIEST, DOMINIC GUZMAN, BURNING THE ALBIGENSIAN BOOKS. CONTRARY TO NORMAL PRACTICE, THE ARRESTS AND ACCUSATIONS OF THE TEMPLARS WERE DIRECTLY SANCTIONED BY THE PAPAL INQUISITOR.

A MEDIEVAL ILLUSTRATION
SHOWING THE STRAPPADO, WITH
THE VICTIM'S HANDS TIED BEHIND
HIS BACK AND WEIGHT ATTACHED
TO HIS FEET, BEING MADE READY TO
BE HOISTED BY PULLEY SLOWLY
TOWARD THE CEILING.

THE INQUISITION

The Inquisition came into existence as a direct result of the
Albigensian Crusade. It originated from the thinking of the
fanatical Spanish priest Dominic Guzman, who spent many
years trying to bring the Cathar heretics back into the fold
of the Church. He failed, but his lasting legacy, the
Inquisition, is still, in a somewhat subtler form, in existence
today under the innocuous name of the Congregation for
the Doctrine of the Faith. Today, anyone who comes to its
attention by questioning the infallibility of the doctrine of
the Church and who does not submit to its discipline is
likely to be excommunicated.

In the medieval era, the favored tool of the Inquisition
was torture, but it was limited by papal instruction to being
used only once on each victim. To overcome this obstruction
the inquisitors adjourned the session, to be resumed at a
later date, thus prolonging the agony of the accused. This
allowed them to torture the prisoner repeatedly without
appearing to defy the papal dictat.

A tradition dating from the ninth century forbade the
Church to shed blood. The techniques of the Inquisition were
designed to keep actual bloodshed to a minimum because
to shed blood by lance, sword, or dagger was considered
un-Christian. Thus the methods of torture devised by the

Inquisitors were designed to cause maximum pain and suffering with the minimum of mess, and often just the sight of the instruments of torture led to a confession.

QUESTIONING UNDER TORTURE

During its operations against the Cathars the Inquisition had perfected its techniques in the art of arrest, trial, and torture of its victims. The most common tortures used were the rack and the strappado.

The rack is probably the best known and most notorious of the methods used. It was a simple raised wooden frame with planks placed across, similar to the rungs of a ladder. The victim's wrists and ankles were attached to rollers at each end. While the prisoner was being questioned, the rollers were turned, tightening the rack until the victim's body was stretched to breaking point.

THE STRAPPADO

The strappado, the preferred method of the torturers, was a form of pulley torture. The victim was stripped to his underwear, his hands were tied behind his back, and his ankles shackled. Another rope tied to his wrists was run over a pulley attached to the ceiling. Iron weights were attached to his feet, then the accused was hoisted above the floor and left dangling from his wrists. In this uncomfortable position the prisoner was whipped while his interrogation continued.

If he was uncooperative his body was hoisted higher then allowed to drop suddenly but prevented from hitting the ground. He was then hoisted up again and the whole process repeated, with the result that severe dislocations were common.

One Templar knight, 50-year-old Gerard de Pasagio, claimed he was tortured "by the hanging of weights on [his] genitals and other members."

THE STIVALETTO

A boot-type of torture, known as the stivaletto or brodequins, involved two thick boards being attached to each of the prisoner's legs with strong rope and tied as tightly as possible. The boards were then forced apart by the

insertion of wooden or metal wedges between them and the legs until the pressure became intolerable and the ropes began to cut into the victim's flesh, or until the sound of splintering bones was heard. Inevitably the prisoner, if he survived, was permanently disabled.

WATER AND FIRE

Another method forced the victim to swallow copious quantities of water, either by means of a funnel or a piece of fabric forced into his throat. The liquid would be continuously dripped into his mouth with the result that often blood vessels would burst from being overhydrated.

An ordeal by fire entailed manacling the prisoner, then coating his feet with fat or grease. He was placed before a roaring fire so that his feet literally fried. The feet of Bernard de Vaho, a Templar priest from the city of Albi, were so badly burned that after a few days the bones dropped out of them.

The tortures used against the Templars achieved almost 100 percent success, for records show that, of the 138 depositions from the hearings that took place in Paris in 1307, only four victims were able to resist. Results from the rest of France were similar.

ARRESTS IN OTHER COUNTRIES

Pope Clement had neither the will nor the power to reverse the king's orders to arrest the Templars. He attempted to regain control by issuing a papal directive to all Christian rulers on November 22, 1307 instructing them to arrest the Templars in their realms and confiscate the order's property.

On hearing of the first arrests in France the English king replied that he could not give "easy credence" to the charges and wrote letters to the kings of Portugal, Castile, Aragon, and Naples. The papal directive left him with no option but to comply with the pope's instructions, however, and he replied that action would be taken against the Templars "in the quickest and best way." The Templars were permitted to remain in their commanderies and few were actually arrested. Initially the use of torture was forbidden in England, so there were no confessions of heresy. However, in June 1311, one Templar, Stephen de Stapelbrugge, confessed to denying Christ and claimed that homosexuality had been encouraged within the order. Under papal

THE DEATH OF JACQUES DE MOLAY, THE LAST GRAND MASTER, AND GEOFFROI DE CHARNEY, ON THE ISLE DES JAVIAUX, IN 1314.

pressure and ecclesiastical law the use of torture was sanctioned, leading to further confessions.

In Portugal the knights were found "not guilty"; in Scotland the verdict was "not proven"; in Spain the archbishop of Compostela wrote to the pope pleading for clemency for the Templars because they were needed in the ongoing fight against the Moors. In Lombardy some bishops who favored the Templars claimed they could find no incriminating evidence. Other countries found them guilty and they were convicted. In Greece and Germany the results were equally varied.

THE DEATH OF JACQUES DE MOLAY

Jacques de Molay was subjected to torture and interrogation for a period of seven years. Then, on March 18, 1314, he was led to an area in front of the cathedral of Notre-Dame de Paris, where the archbishop of Sens and three papal commissioners were seated on a specially erected stage. The bishop of Alba read out the confessions of the four leading Templars and pronounced a sentence of life imprisonment on them. Jacques de Molay intervened and was allowed to speak on the assumption that he was about to confess his guilt. He spoke thus:

It is just that, in so terrible a day, and in the last moments of my life, I should discover all the iniquity of falsehood, and make the triumph, I declare, then, in the face of heaven and earth, and acknowledge, though to my eternal shame, that I have committed the greatest of crimes but ... it had been the acknowledging of those which have been so foully charged on the Order. I attest—and truth obliges me to attest—that it is innocent! I made contrary declaration only to suspend the excessive pains of torture, and to mollify those who made me endure them. I know the punishments which have been inflicted on all the knights who had the courage to revoke a similar confession; but the dreadful spectacle which is presented to me is not able to make me confirm one lie by another. The life offered me on such infamous terms I abandon without regret.

THE CHARGES AGAINST THE TEMPLARS

THIS LIST DETAILS THE MAIN CHARGES BROUGHT AGAINST THE TEMPLARS FOLLOWING THEIR ARREST IN OCTOBER 1307:

✤ THAT DURING THE RECEPTION CEREMONY, NEW BROTHERS WERE REQUIRED TO DENY CHRIST, GOD, THE VIRGIN, OR THE SAINTS ON THE COMMAND OF THOSE RECEIVING THEM.

✤ THAT THE BROTHERS COMMITTED VARIOUS SACRILEGIOUS ACTS—TRAMPLING, SPITTING, URINATING—EITHER ON THE CROSS OR ON AN IMAGE OF CHRIST.

✤ THAT THE RECEPTORS PRACTICED OBSCENE KISSES ON NEW ENTRANTS, ON THE MOUTH, NAVEL, BASE OF THE SPINE, OR BUTTOCKS.

✤ THAT TEMPLAR PRIESTS DID NOT CONSECRATE THE HOST, AND THAT THE BROTHERS DID NOT BELIEVE IN THE SACRAMENTS.

✤ THAT THE BROTHERS PRACTICED IDOL WORSHIP OF A CAT OR A HEAD, CALLED BAPHOMET.

✤ THAT THE BROTHERS PRACTICED INSTITUTIONAL SODOMY.

✤ THAT THE GRAND MASTER, OR OTHER HIGH-RANKING OFFICIALS, ABSOLVED FELLOW TEMPLARS OF THEIR SINS.

✤ THAT THE TEMPLARS HELD THEIR RECEPTION CEREMONIES AND CHAPTER MEETINGS IN SECRET AND AT NIGHT.

✤ THAT THE TEMPLARS ABUSED THE DUTIES OF CHARITY AND HOSPITALITY AND USED ILLEGAL MEANS TO ACQUIRE PROPERTY AND INCREASE THEIR WEALTH.

The preceptor of Normandy, Geoffroi de Charney, stood beside the Grand Master to show his support, revoked his former confession, and also spoke of the sanctity of the order. Proceedings were stopped and the papal commissioners issued orders to clear the square, then rushed to report to the king who immediately condemned the two to a most horrific death. By retracting their confessions they were now relapsed heretics and there was only one punishment that would fit this crime—death by fire. The execution took place on the Isle des Javiaux the next day, when the knights were roasted over a hot, smokeless fire, ensuring that they died slowly. Before he died, Jacques de Molay cursed the pope and the king and called on them both to appear before God within the year. His words proved to be prophetic, for Pope Clement died on April 20, to be followed on November 29, by King Philippe.

the templars after 1307

AFTER THE SUPPRESSION OF THEIR ORDER, THE TEMPLAR KNIGHTS WHO ESCAPED
ARREST FLED TO DIFFERENT COUNTRIES AND SEEMED TO DISAPPEAR. HOWEVER,
THE TEMPLAR AND REX DEUS TRADITIONS WERE KEPT ALIVE BY THE GRAIL SAGAS
AND RE-EMERGED WITH THE DEVELOPMENT OF FREEMASONRY.

trange to relate, the Order of the Knights Templar was never actually condemned for heresy by the papacy. Yet, on March 22, 1312, a papal bull, *Vox in Excelso*, was issued announcing the dissolution of the order because it had "fallen into disrepute." As head of the Church, the pope claimed spiritual and temporal authority over all rulers, and his edicts, promulgated as papal bulls, could be issued on any matter at any time at his prerogative. They were not necessarily or even usually associated with condemnation. More often they gave protection, status, and recognition to clerical orders, knightly orders, and individuals. The Order of the Poor Knights of the Temple of Solomon may have ceased to exist after the official dissolution, but the knights themselves did not. Friday, October 13, 1307, had seen the arrest of only 620 members of the Templar Order, not all of whom were knights. According to most historians, the total number of brothers in France prior to that date was in the region of 3,000. What happened to those who escaped the clutches of the arresting officers? The fate of many ex-Templars can be established from the records of pensions paid to them in different countries either by the state or the Church. Most joined other military or religious orders, including the many descendants of the 24 ma'madot, namely the Rex Deus families, and the surviving members of the inner circles of the Templar hierarchy. These family members turned adversity to advantage by joining other military orders, where they rapidly rose to positions of power and influence as a result of their bravery and talent.

OTHER MILITARY ORDERS

Some of the fleeing Templars joined the Knights Hospitaller, their one-time rivals in the Holy Land; others joined the Teutonic Knights. Both of these orders were aware of the winds of change after the fall of Acre when it became obvious that their role as warriors was no longer enough,

---

THE ORDER OF MONTESA

THE ORDER OF MONTESA WAS SET UP BY KING JAMES II OF ARAGON WHO GAVE THEM THE CASTLE OF THAT NAME. THE ORDER RECEIVED OTHER PROPERTIES, ALTHOUGH THEIR OWNERSHIP OF SOME WAS DISPUTED. APPROVAL FOR THE NEW KNIGHTLY ORDER WAS GIVEN BY POPE JOHN XXII ON JUNE 10, 1317. THE ORDER WAS GIVEN THE CISTERCIAN RULE AND LIMITED TO OPERATING IN THE KINGDOM OF ARAGON UNDER THE ORDERS OF THE KING. THE ORDER OF MONTESA SUPPORTED THE KING IN CIVIL WARS, BUT WAS ONLY MARGINALLY INVOLVED IN THE RECONQUISTA AGAINST THE MOORS.

---

and they had to change their focus in order to survive. The Teutonic Knights concentrated on fighting the pagans in Eastern Europe and even founded their own state of Prussia. The Hospitallers acquired the islands of Malta and Rhodes, and altered their mission to suppressing the Saracen pirates.

The fate of the Templars in Portugal was somewhat different, for King Diniz had found the Templars innocent, so they simply changed their name to the Knights of Christ and continued under royal patronage from their headquarters at Tomar. This order was recognized by Pope John XXII in 1319, in the papal bull *Ad ea ex Quibus*. The regulations for new entrants were changed, restricting membership to nobles of Portuguese birth, and the order continued for another two centuries.

In Spain the Archbishop of Compostela begged in vain that the Templars be spared, giving as his reason the need for their services in the ongoing fight against the Moors in the Reconquista and, as a result, ex-Templars with their military expertise, dedication, and discipline were encouraged to join other local military orders that owed allegiance to the Spanish crown rather than to the pope, such as the Knights of Alcantara and the Knights of Santiago. The latter were affiliated to the Knights Hospitaller in order to ensure their survival. In the kingdom of Aragon the Templars became members of either the Knights of Calatrava (the oldest military order in the Iberian Peninsula) or another founded by King James II, the Order of Montesa, which was made up entirely of ex-Templars. In France and England some Templars joined the Hospitallers, but most of them simply seemed to vanish.

A FIFTEENTH-CENTURY PAINTING BY THE SPANISH SCHOOL OF OUR LADY OF GRACE AND THE MASTERS OF THE ORDER OF MONTESA. THE MASTERS' WHITE MANTLES BEAR THE SAME RED CROSS ON A WHITE MANTLE AS THAT WORN BY THE TEMPLARS.

TEMPLARS IN SCOTLAND

Many Templars fled to Scotland for, in 1314, the entire country was under papal interdict, making it the one country in Europe where they were safe from the pope's writ. A bitter conflict had arisen between claimants for the crown of Scotland. Robert the Bruce, the main contender, had been excommunicated for the murder of his rival John Comyn on church premises. When the papal decree was ignored by the entire Scottish nobility, they too fell foul of the pope and were excommunicated; the rest of the population soon followed suit.

The renegade Templar knights offered their services to Robert the Bruce and fought in the battle that finally ended the civil war and secured the crown for Bruce, the Battle of Bannockburn in 1314. According to Prince Michael of Albany, "432 Templar knights ... routed the English invader and preserved Scottish independence." The Rex Deus tradition tells how Robert the Bruce became sovereign Grand Master of the Templar Order as an act of gratitude and recognition.

Only two Templars were ever tried in Scotland, and the trial judge Bishop Lamberton brought in the Scottish verdict of "not proven," but this was not enough to protect the order as a whole. The new king, recognizing the need to make his peace with the pope, warned the knights to go underground. Henceforth, Templar properties in Scotland passed into the keeping of the Knights Hospitaller; however, these properties were always accounted for separately as if they were being held in trust until such time as they could be returned to their rightful owners.

THE TEMPLAR TREASURE

After the initial arrests in France, the king's seneschals raided the Paris Temple—but in vain. The treasure brought by Jacques de Molay that King Philippe had seen being carried into the building had vanished, along with the Templar fleet of 18 ships that had left La Rochelle. One uncorroborated story states that an unspecified amount was taken northward to Belgium in a cart covered in hay. Historians Stephen Dafoe and Alan Butler claim that much of the treasure was transported east to Switzerland, where the Templars owned considerable property. They propose that the knights went underground but used their financial acumen to found the Swiss banking system. Another theory is offered by French Masonic tradition. According to this, the treasure was destined for Scotland, and ended up in the hands of the St. Clairs of Roslin. The St. Clairs, who were already wealthy, suddenly became "super rich." From then on, the Lords St. Clair of Roslin were escorted by 400 mounted knights when they rode abroad, their ladies were attended by 80 ladies-in-waiting, and they were reputed to have dined off gold plate. The fortunes of the family continued to grow. The Third Earl of Orkney and Baron of Roslin, William St. Clair, the builder of Rosslyn Chapel, was renowned for his incredible wealth.

THE RISE OF FREEMASONRY

In his book *Born in Blood*, the American historian John Robinson explores in depth the help given by the lodges of craftmasons to the Templars who fled after the initial wave of arrests in France. Links between the dissolved order and various craftmasons' guilds can be made in many countries, but it is in Scotland that they are most obvious, for it is here that the guilds eventually developed into Freemasonry.

Under the guidance of the St. Clairs of Rosslyn, the hidden members of the Templar Order selected suitable candidates from the operative craft guilds to receive instruction in various branches of esoteric knowledge, which included science, geometry, history, philosophy, and the contents of the scrolls possibly discovered by the Templars under the Temple Mount in Jerusalem. This new brotherhood of "free" Masons created charitable institutions that supported the poorer members of society, the first such institutions to be set up that were not within the direct control of the Church.

The first three centuries of Freemasonry were shrouded in secrecy, making it difficult now to assess all the esoteric influences that formed it. The prime movers behind the transformation of the guilds of operative Masons into Freemasonry were almost certainly the Templars. In Scotland, where ordinary workers were admitted in large numbers, the tradition of preserving sacred knowledge through teaching rituals remained almost intact, reaching a high degree of sophistication and complexity. Ultimately this led to the development of the Royal Arch Degrees and Scottish Rite Freemasonry, which was founded on the principles enunciated in the Declaration of Arbroath in 1320, and which was later incorporated into a formal constitution for Scottish Rite Freemasonry. French lodges preserved the original esoteric teaching as much as possible, and maintained close links with their brothers in

Scotland, an association that is recorded in the rite of "Strict Observance," which reports that speculative Masons from operative lodges of the Compannonage in France visited the lodge at Aberdeen in 1361.

There is one degree in the rites of Freemasonry that commemorates the foundation of the Order of the Templars, that of the "Knight of the East and West." The ritual states that it was first promulgated during the crusades in 1118, when 11 knights took a vow of secrecy, friendship, and discretion under the supervision of the patriarch of Jerusalem. The two additional knights to the original nine founders are Count Fulk of Anjou and Hughes I of Champagne. The principle of sevenfoldedness found in

RIGHT: SIR WILLIAM ST. CLAIR OF ROSSLYN, THE LAST HEREDITARY GRAND MASTER OF FREEMASONRY IN SCOTLAND, WHO RESIGNED HIS HEREDITARY POSITION IN 1736.

THE ST. CLAIR FAMILY WERE INSTRUMENTAL IN DEVELOPING FREEMASONRY IN SCOTLAND AFTER MANY TEMPLAR CRAFTMASONS HAD FLED THERE FROM FRANCE.

this degree underpins the symbolism of the Revelation of St. John the Evangelist, who, with John the Baptist, was of supreme importance in the Templar belief system.

THE RAMSAY ORATION

Andrew Michael Ramsay was a graduate of the University of Edinburgh in the early eighteenth century. He fled to France in 1710, where he converted to Catholicism. A number of posts, first under the Duc de Chateau-Thierry and later the Prince of Turenne, led to him being made a Knight of the Order of St. Lazarus. Chevalier Ramsay's first loyalty was to the Stuart king in exile, known to the people of Scotland as "the king over the water." Ramsay went to Rome in 1724,

BELOW: A LATE-EIGHTEENTH-CENTURY ILLUSTRATION OF A THIRD DEGREE MASONIC INITIATION, MOST PROBABLY UNDER THE AUSPICES OF GRAND ORIENT OF FRANCE.

as tutor to Prince Charles Edward Stuart, and was involved in efforts to restore him to the throne of Scotland. When he returned to France he took an active role in French Freemasonry and set about transforming the movement. Ramsay proclaimed that Freemasonry had its origins in the crusades to liberate the Holy Land, although he had no evidence to back up these claims. What he did have was credibility and authority as a result of his posts: he was Chancellor of the Grand Lodge of Paris, a Chevalier of the Order of St. Lazarus, one-time tutor of Prince Charles, and a one-time member of the Royal Society, which all lent credence to his reliability.

ALMANACH
DES
COCUS,
OU
AMUSEMENS
Pour le beau Sexe.

POUR L'ANNE'E M. DCC. XLI.

Auquel on a joint un recueil de Pieces
fur les Francs-Maçons.

Ouvrage Inftructif, Epigrammatique, &
Enigmatique, dedié à la Jeuneffe
amoureufe.

Par un Philofophe Garçon.

A CONSTANTINOPLE,
De l'Imprimerie du GRAND SEIGNEUR

M. DCC. XLI.
Avec Approbation des Sultanes.

At the Masonic Lodge of St. Thomas in Paris he delivered a speech that stunned his fellow Masons because in it he claimed that Freemasonry had its true origins among the kings, princes, knights, and nobility of the crusades and not the unlettered craftmasons of the medieval era:

Our ancestors, the crusaders, gathered together from all parts of Christendom in the Holy Land, desired thus to reunite into one sole Fraternity the individuals of all nations …

He claimed that the original knightly Masons of the crusades were men who had sworn to rebuild the temple of God on earth in the Holy Land, not workers in stone as was commonly believed. He asserted that, on their return to Europe, the crusaders had established lodges in France, Italy, Spain, Germany, and Scotland and that the Lord Steward of Scotland was Grand Master of the Lodge at Kilwinning in 1286. He further claimed that every country except Scotland had neglected the early lodges, making his own country the originator of Freemasonry where it had continued in an unbroken line since the crusades. The Oration by Chevalier Ramsay led to a veritable tidal wave of Masonic activity across France. All who had any pretensions to chivalry or fraternity flocked to become members. As a result of Ramsay's acknowledgment of Freemasonry's Scottish roots, one French system that was influenced by supporters of the Stuart cause gained the name "Scottish Rite Freemasonry," a "new" form that had 33 degrees of initiation.

THE RITE OF STRICT OBSERVANCE
In 1743, a German nobleman, Baron von Hund, was initiated into a form of Freemasonry that required his absolute obedience to certain unspecified and unknown superiors. Entries in his diary show that he was received

LEFT: THE *ALMANACH DES COCUS*, 1741, PRINTED RAMSAY'S FAMOUS SPEECH IN WHICH HE CITED THE CRUSADERS AS THE TRUE ANCESTORS OF THE FREEMASONS.

ABOVE RIGHT: A PAINTING OF AN INITIATION CEREMONY IN A VIENNESE MASONIC LODGE, 1784. MOZART IS SEATED ON THE EXTREME LEFT OF THE PICTURE.

into this Masonic Order by an unknown official who bore the title "Knight of the Red Feather." He was welcomed as "a distinguished brother," then told the "true story" of the origins of Freemasonry, which was disclosed at his initiation. According to this, after the suppression of the Templar Order a group of knights had sought refuge in Scotland, where they joined a guild of working masons and in this way kept their order going. They had chosen a successor to Jacques de Molay, and the order had continued from that day, governed by an unbroken succession of Grand Masters. Each Grand Master's name was known only to those who elected him, thus maintaining the secrecy of the order; hence the strange oath of absolute obedience to an unknown superior.

Von Hund was instructed to return to Germany, set up lodges of the Rite of Strict Observance and await further instructions. He took his role very seriously, and founded

lodges that not only spread throughout Germany and the rest of Europe but also found their way to North America, where they took root and flourished across the continent. He never had any further contact with his unknown superiors, and was apparently deserted by them. The Knight of the Red Feather seemed to vanish. In fact, both the Knight of the Red Feather and those present at Von Hund's acceptance ceremony had all been killed in the Jacobite rebellion of 1745.

Six years after Von Hund's death, a convention of "reformed" Masonic groups was held at Willhelmsbad. The baron's claims were rejected, although lodges belonging to the original Strict Observance continued. Another system, the Rectified Scottish Rite—the Rite of Strict Observance by a new name—which downplayed the Templar connection, was approved by those at Willhelmsbad. Although small compared with other Masonic systems, this is still in existence today, in particular in France.

THE CHARTER OF LARMENIUS

In 1804, documents were allegedly discovered that were then used in support of a claim of continuous Templar survival. A document known as the Charter of Larmenius was used by Bernard-Raymond de Fabré-Palaprat to substantiate the legitimacy of the neo-Templar Order he had created with his cofounder Philippe Ledru. The charter, supposedly dated 1324, claims that shortly before his execution Jacques de Molay nominated a Templar in Cyprus, Jean-Marc Larmenius, as his successor, and that the Templars had continued in secret after the suppression. Fabré-Palaprat used this to support his claim that a non-Masonic chivalric order was still in existence that was the direct heir of the Templars. This order, "the Ancient and Sovereign Military Order of the Temple of Jerusalem," is still extant.

Whether or not the Charter of Larmenius is authentic has been the subject of considerable dispute among historians ever since its alleged "discovery." Three dates have been suggested for this—1364, 1705, and 1805—but, whichever is correct, it seems that the author was admitting the survival of the Templar Order in Scotland.

As true Gnostics, the controlling Templars concerned themselves with the spiritual and material transformation of entire communities and nations, unlike the Church, whose only concern was the salvation of individual souls. With the demise of the Templars, Rex Deus had to continue to observe the religion of the community in which they lived and moved and to bide their time until another opportunity to bring their beliefs and traditions into the open presents itself.

EUROPE TRANSFORMED

Why did the Knights Templar have such a profound influence on European culture in the medieval era rather than any other order, military or religious? The answer to that question remains a mystery. Many accounts compare the order with others of the time, but only in the military field. The Templars had a transformative effect on the peace and stability of Europe far greater than any other order, and played a part in setting the scene for the rise of capitalism. Their use of the fruits of their esoteric knowledge for the good of the community went far beyond the realms of brotherhood within the order, being extended to the general populace.

So it appears likely that the true reason behind the resounding success of the Templar Order and its meteoric rise to power in both the military and political fields derived from the application of their "heretical" belief system to the world in which they lived. The heritage they have left us is encoded within medieval Church art and sacred geometry at places such as Chartres and Amiens Cathedrals and smaller churches across Europe and the Middle East; within Christian iconography that has hidden messages encoded within it, such as the Black Madonna, as well as the deliberate omission of scenes of the Crucifixion. It can be found in the Templar seals of office, such as the two brothers on one horse and the Abraxus; and within the Grail sagas, which were described by the internationally renowned scholar Professor Joseph Campbell as coded guides to a spiritual pathway of enlightenment.

Yet the Templars were condemned as heretics and suppressed. The concepts of brotherhood, loyalty, integrity, and service to others that were a fundamental part of the Templar beliefs were continued with the formation of the Freemasons and the Rosicrucians, both of which continued the traditions begun by the knights, and who played such a pivotal role in the formation of modern European society.

THE INTERIOR OF THE TEMPLE CHURCH IN LONDON, WHICH WAS COMPLETED IN 1185. AFTER THE DESTRUCTION AND ABOLITION OF THE TEMPLAR ORDER THE CHURCH WAS HANDED OVER TO THE KNIGHTS HOSPITALLER BY EDWARD II.

GLOSSARY

Abraxas, the One of the seals used by the Grand Masters of the Knights Templar on documents classed as "confidential" or "top-secret." It always contains Gnostic symbolism and may have given rise to the magical expression abracadabra; in medieval times "abraxas stones" carved with Cabbalistic symbols were often the prized possessions of alchemists.

Albigensians Residents of the city of Albi in Languedoc, a center of the Cathar movement. The city became the focus of the so-called Albigensian Crusade, which was called in order to root out and destroy all followers of the Cathar tradition, both in Albi and through southwest France.

Apsidal churches Rectangular churches with a rounded recess or "bay window area," at the eastern end of the aisle that often contained the main altar or, in larger churches, a secondary chapel.

Ark of the Covenant Originally, the strongbox or chest in which the tablets of stone containing the Ten Commandments were kept. Regarded by Moses and the people of Israel as most holy.

Baphomet Name or title of an idol which the Knights Templar were accused of worshipping in place of God; no derivation or explanation of the name is known, and it is of uncertain provenance.

Barons of Roslin and the Earls of Orkney The St. Clairs, a Norman French family, were granted land around Roslin, Scotland, by Malcolm Canmore in 1068 when William de St. Clair accompanied the Saxon princess Margaret north to her marriage with the Scottish king. Later St. Clairs (now more commonly Sinclairs) became the Earls of Orkney, the first of whom, Earl Henry St. Clair, according to family legend for which there is considerable proof on both sides of the Atlantic, led an expedition to North America in 1398 almost a century before Columbus and some 50 years before the founding of Rosslyn Chapel.

Benedictine monks Monks who follow the Rule established by Benedict of Nursia (c. 530 CE) who built many churches and abbeys in the Romanesque style.

Bernard of Clairvaux Abbot of the French Cistercian abbey of Clairvaux during the early twelfth century, who was highly influential in both spiritual and temporal matters being the adviser to two popes and various kings and emperors. His main focus was on Mariolatry, initiatory spirituality, and the promotion of the Second Crusade.

Black Madonnas Statues and iconlike paintings of the Madonna and child in which the Madonna is depicted as dark or black; most date from the eleventh to fifteenth centuries and are located in churches and shrines particularly associated with the Templars; the Madonna depicted may therefore represent Mary Magdalene with the son she bore Jesus, an heretical belief prevalent at the time, or the Egyptian deity of Isis with the Horus child.

Byzantium Name not just for the major city re-established by Constantine the Great in 330 CE, but for the Eastern Roman (or Byzantine) Empire of which it was the capital until 1453, when the city fell to the Ottoman Turks and was later renamed as Istanbul.

Cabbala Also spelled Kabbalah, Kabbala and Qabbala (among other variants), became the principal mystical movement within Judaism that was intended to elicit and use esoteric knowledge of God and his Creation, with particular reference to finding special meaning in the words of the Tanakh (the Hebrew Bible); some Cabbalist scholars focus entirely on numerological interpretations.

Caliph Arabic word generally translated as "successor," but meaning the head of an Islamic state or region, whether by appointment or by patrimony, as the local successor to the Prophet Muhammad. The title was formally abolished in 1924.

Capetian kings Kings of France who descended directly from Hugh Capet, Count of Paris (died 996 CE), until 1328 (death of Charles IV of France). From 1328 to 1830 France was ruled by the Valois and Bourbon branches of the same family.

Cathars Dualists who lived in society as "pure ones" (Greek katharoi) and who lived much of their lives as credentes "believers" before undergoing "baptism of the Spirit" in a ceremony known as consolamentum, and thus becoming perfecti, the equivalent of highly ascetic clergy; that in due course anyone and everyone could become perfecti meant that they saw no need for a formal priesthood. They lived predominantly in southwest France, Provence, and northern Italy.

Christendom The area in which Christianity, under the authority of the pope, was the sole religion.

Cistercian Order The Cistercian Order was formed in an endeavor both to revert to the original Rule of St. Benedict and to increase the austerity of the required lifestyle with particular reference to manual labor. Its principal mentor and theologian was Bernard of Clairvaux.

Cohens (of ancient Israel) Priests of the family of Moses' brother Aaron, a hereditary priestly order from which were chosen all the legitimate High Priests of the Jewish Temple in Jerusalem. Derived from the leading members of the Tribe of Levi, their prestige is considerable among Orthodox and Conservative Jews of today.

Consolamentum The ritual laying-on of hands in the Cathar rite that corresponded to "baptism by the Holy Spirit" initiating a perfectus; it was the beginning of the formal initiatory process that continued for a lifetime as the perfectus ascends through the degrees of enlightenment, receiving increasing levels of spiritual knowledge.

Coptic Describing the form of Christianity by tradition ascribed to the missionary endeavor of St. Mark in first-century Egypt and, since the Council of Chalcedon (451 CE) part of the Eastern Orthodox Church; the head of the Church is styled the Pope of Alexandria, Patriarch of the Holy See of St. Mark; more than 95 percent of Christians in Egypt today belong to this Church, although there is also a Greek Orthodox Patriarch of Alexandria and a "Coptic Catholic" Patriarch.

Croix fleury An equalled armed cross in which the ends are surmounted with the fleur-de-lys. Symbolic of the Rex Deus families, it is now the blazon of the chivalric Order of the Fleur-de-Lys.

Croix pattée This form of cross has four arms of equal length but of increasing thickness from the center (like a Maltese cross or a military Iron Cross), whether curved or straight; a red cross pattée became the official symbol of the Knights Templar from 1128, and was much in evidence during the Crusades. The name comes from the thickening arms of the cross, which seemed like paws (Norman French *pattes*).

Desposyni Descendants of the family of Jesus Christ and Mary Magdalene; the term derives from Greek and literally means "(those) of the Lord," and was applied also to the early followers of Jesus who resisted attempts to turn the Church away from the Jewish-based teaching of Jesus and toward the philosophy advocated by Paul.

Diaspora Greek for "dispersal," "scattering," but used (with a capital letter) particularly to refer to the scattering of Israelites/Jews first following the destruction of the Temple by the Babylonians in 586 BCE and then following the destruction of Jerusalem by the Romans in 70 and 136 CE; as diaspora (with a lower-case initial letter) the word refers to ethnic and religious groups—particularly the Jewish people—scattered among other peoples and nations.

Dualism Philosophical and religious system by which everything has its opposite. There cannot be one single God who is all-goodness unless there is another deity who is all-evil; some dualist elements exist in Christianity, notably the distinction between God as the bringer of Light and the Devil as the Master of Darkness; the oldest recorded truly dualist religion is Zoroastrianism.

El Khidir See **Khidir, El**.

Essenes Members of a large and influential sect among the Jews at the time of Jesus and for a century before his birth. Apparently founded by the ma'madot, the hereditary high priestly families who rejected Temple worship after a non-member was appointed as a High Priest. They were an apocalyptic and initiatory sect who were governed by "the Teacher of Righteousness" and were dedicated to strict purity and "doing Torah," i.e. absolute adherence to the Law of Moses. The Nazoreans are known to have been an offshoot of the Essenes.

Excommunication Originally, total ostracization of an individual by his or her local church by order of the senior Catholic clergy, as a punishment for disagreement with Church dogma or a serious violation. Sentence was tantamount to a sentence of eternal death as opposed to the eternal life as proffered by the Church, which still issues excommunication orders today.

Freemasons Fraternal association or brotherhood based partly on metaphysical ideals but retaining essentially esoteric and secret rituals of initiation and internal advance; there is a constitutional declaration of belief in a Supreme Being, but the fraternity holds dear a symbolic relationship with operative stonemasonry, its tools and methods; the main aims of the "Craft" are the growing spiritual enlightenment of its members and the social and psychological progress of people in general.

Gentiles Originally, people who were not Jewish and who were therefore "of (another) race" (Latin *gentilis*).

Gnosticism, Gnostic thought Esoteric compilation of occult knowledge of divine origin (gnosis) which sprang from various early religions and mystery cults; a form of religion that recognized a hierarchy of deities that was influential on early Christian thought.

Gospel of Thomas, the Collection of the sayings of Jesus (including a few "dialogues") discovered at Nag Hammadi that is often described as a Gnostic document but most probably dates from a time before Gnosticism had genuinely influenced Christian thought. Many of the "sayings" recorded within it have no known parallel in the canonical New Testament, and some are actually contradictory. Regarded by many scholars as a more accurate reflection of the true teachings of Jesus than that found in the Canonical Gospels.

Gothic architecture Style of formal building in Europe between the twelfth and the sixteenth centuries, characterized by interior height featuring pointed arches, pillars, and rib vaulting. Its high walls supported by flying buttresses allowed far greater window spaces. In England, Gothic architecture begins as Early English, moves through Decorated, and ends as Perpendicular.

Grand Master Title of the supreme head of many Orders of knighthood, it is also the title of some master craftsmen among medieval guilds or similar fraternal organizations, such as the modern Freemasons.

Hassidim The "Holy Ones" among the Jews, people who, from very early on in Jewish history, dedicated themselves to strict religious observance and were first mentioned in the Bible at the time of the Maccabean revolt. Modern use of the term Hassidim generally refers to those Jews who follow the teachings of Rabbi Ba'al Shem Tov (Rabbi Israel ben Eliezer, c. 1750) and concentrate on expressing two fundamentally immediate religious and social notions that God is omnipresent, and that God and humans interact.

Holy Grail, the The ultimate objective of those who quest after religious purity or initiatory spirituality. It has been described, in allegorical terms, as the chalice or cup (Old French *graal*) used at the Last Supper, and has also been held to symbolize the "holy blood" (medieval French *sang réal*) of Jesus and his descendants. According to Professor Joseph Campbell, the true Holy Grail is initiatory spiritual enlightenment.

Holy Roman Emperors Rulers of a widespread but often-changing territory within Europe between 800 and 1806, and crowned as such by the contemporary pope thus, incidentally, affirming the pope's temporal authority. The first Holy Roman Emperor was Charlemagne, King of the Franks. Later, from 1438 onwards, all Holy Roman Emperors were from the House of Habsburg and the last was Emperor Franz I of Austria.

Hughes I, Count of Champagne Count of Champagne, Lord of Troyes, Bar-sur-Aube and Vitry, who encouraged the establishment of a Jewish Cabbalistic school in his realm under the direction of the great Jewish thinker Rabbi Raschi. Hughes was closely involved with the founding of the Order of the Knights Templar and the majority of the early members of that Order were his subjects. He left Champagne to join the Order within a few years of its foundation, leaving his title and worldly possessions to his nephew, Theobald (or Thibaud).

Illuminati, the The "Enlightened ones," those who have achieved the highest level of initiation and are deemed to be "enlightened." Also used in reference to a legendary mystical order often accused of political involvement even today, however, none of the conspiracy theorists who advance such ideas have ever managed to prove that the Order actually exists.

Infidel An unbeliever, as described by a believer of a specific religious faith—particularly, by English literary convention from the nineteenth century, a Christian as described by a Muslim, but in the English of earlier centuries more often a Muslim as described by a Christian.

Initiation cults/orders Associations and groupings in which spiritual knowledge or gnosis is granted to those who ascend through a number of degrees of initiation under the guidance of a spiritual teacher or "hierophant."

Inquisition, the Form of court established by the Catholic Church in 1233 to root out and suppress heretical views; officers of the court held considerable disciplinary powers of investigation and punishment, put to full use notably in Spain between the sixteenth and eighteenth centuries. Its current form has since 1965 been formally called the Sacred Congregation for the Doctrine of the Faith.

Isis cult An initiation cult of the Egyptian goddess Isis devoted to the sacred mysteries leading to the imparting of sacred wisdom. The image of Isis with her son Horus seemed to early Roman Christians to reflect the image of the Virgin Mary with Jesus and may account for some of the Black Madonnas.

Jihad In Arabic literally meaning "struggle," that is one of the prescribed duties of all Muslims toward the promotion of Islamic principles. It is the sacred duty of subduing one's personal ego and deepening one's submission to the "will of God." It can be fulfilled in any or all of four ways—by the heart, by the tongue, by the hand, and by the sword—and thus has led to the concept of "the Holy War."

John the Baptist Allegedly the second cousin of Jesus, in fact an itinerant preacher and baptiser who is now accepted as being an Essene. In Christian theology he was the man who announced the coming of the Messiah; however, to those who follow the hidden streams of spirituality, he was the teacher and initiator of Jesus.

John the Evangelist Writer of the fourth gospel of the New Testament usually identified as "the disciple whom Jesus loved." John, who is regarded as the most enlightened pupil of Jesus, wrote prolifically and his works display distinct Gnostic elements; the secret Gospel of John, also known as "the Gospel of Love" was the only scripture revered by the Cathars.

Joseph of Arimathea Wealthy citizen of Jerusalem whose private mausoleum was the scene of Jesus' resurrection from the dead; it was he who according to one tradition collected some of Jesus' blood while he was on the Cross in a chalice that many believe is the Holy Grail.

Khidir, El Legendary mystical teacher of the Sufi orders. Described in the Holy Qur'an (Koran) as the guide and companion of Moses, as the immortal servant of Allah, a sage, guardian, and guide to all travelers, especially when crossing the sea. El Khidir (or Khidr or Khedir) also has folk associations with fertility for his name, "the verdant one," equates with the Green Man and the May King. According to some scholars he is also conflated with the Christian St. George.

Ma'amadot, the The 24 hereditary families of the High Priests of the Temple in Jerusalem, all drawn from the Cohen clan within the tribe of Levi and who claim a double descent from both Aaron and Zadok the Priest.

Macabees, the Judas Maccabaeus and his four brothers who, rebelling against the Hellenic Seleucid overlords of Judea in 166 BCE, defeated the Seleucids, entered Jerusalem in triumph, and ritually cleansed the Temple—an event that to this day has been commemorated by the Jewish festival of Hanukkah; rule of Israel by the Hasmonean dynasty thereafter lasted for around a century until between 63 and 37 BCE.

Mandylion, the The mystical image of Jesus' face imprinted upon a cloth, said to have been sent by Jesus to Abgarus of Edessa to heal him of a disability. Some 450 years later an image of similar description was discovered in Edessa and was hailed as miraculous, only to be lost during the Persian conquest of the area in 609; by tradition it surfaced once more in the 940s and was taken to Constantinople amid rejoicing; however, it was finally, supposedly, lost at the sack of that city by the crusaders in 1204. The Vatican now claims to have possession of it.

Manor Large or even stately house suitable as a residence for the local lord or squire; introduced into English by the Norman French the word originally meant no more than "stopping place," or "locality."

Muhammad, the Great Prophet The spiritually gifted prophet to whom the Holy Qur'an was dictated by the archangel Gabriel. The Holy Qur'an did not take its present written form until after his death in 632 CE. Muhammad is recognized by the adherents of Islam as the last and greatest of God's prophets in the sequence listed in the Hebrew Bible, a list that also includes Jesus as one of his predecessors. According to Muhammad, he was not sent to start a new religion, but to bring people back to the true monotheism that had existed since time immemorial. In Islamic tradition Adam was the first Muslim.

Nazoreans, the An offshoot of the Essenes. The description of Jesus as a Nazarene, or as "of Nazareth," was undoubtedly intended to disguise his belonging to this sect and following a spiritual path that predates Christianity.

Papal states Territories within central Italy under the direct, personal rule of the pope between 756 and 1870 (when Italy became a unified country).

Paul (Saul of Tarsus) Self-appointed Christian apostle whose ideas and methods transformed the Jewish-oriented beliefs of the true disciples of Jesus and laid the theological foundations for early Christianity. Paul was a well-educated Roman citizen, a member of the Herodian Royal family with friends in the Roman Emperor's household. Regarded by Church historians as "the father of Christianity" and by adherents of the hidden stream of spirituality, as well as the followers of Jesus, as "the spouter of lies" and "the distorter of the true teachings of Jesus," Paul was, most probably, the first Christian heretic.

Pectoral Large chain or metal ornament intended to hang on and over the chest, generally from the neck; a cross or crucifix that hangs on or over the chest in this way is accordingly called a pectoral cross (as worn particularly by Christian bishops); in medieval times, many pectoral crosses were made to hold what purported to be relics of the True Cross.

Reconquista Generally, the gradual reconquest of Moorish Spain by the Christian kingdoms of northern Spain between 722 CE (the Battle of Covadonga) and 1492 (the final surrender of Granada); however, the term is used also of the reconquest of Portugal from the Moors, which ended in 1249.

Rex Deus Name (meaning "king god") of the European branch of the descendants of the ma'madot which includes the descendants of Jesus and Mary Magdalene.

Richard I, "the Lionheart," King of England At his accession aged 32 in 1189, the eldest surviving son of Henry II, Richard was already famous for military brilliance—mostly in crushing baronial revolts in his territories in France that were far more important to him than England (a country in which he spent no more than a total of ten months during his lifetime). It was his many years of warfare during the

Crusades that spurred Richard to insist that St. George become England's patron saint, although formal acceptance of St. George as patron saint was only ratified in 1415, over 100 years after Richard's death in 1199.

Rosicrucians A loose-knit group of seventeenth-century philosophers who made use of alchemical terms and ideas and claims of occult powers. The true founder was, most probably, the pastor Johann Valentin Andrea whose work was allegedly founded on the teaching of a figure known as Christian Rosenkreutz—hence the name Rosicrucians.

St. George Soldier thought to have been martyred as a Christian in Lydda, Palestine, in the very early fourth century, and described as such by Western European historians of the seventh and eighth centuries; but during the First Crusade, a vision of Saints George and Demetrius preceded the defeat of the Saracens at Antioch, and George then became patron saint of soldiers, and especially Christian soldiers; 100 years later still, the story of his battle with a dragon (and incidental rescue of a princess) was first recorded.

St. Michael the Archangel A saint of great importance to the Knights Templar, the leader of the "heavenly host" against the forces of the Devil (or dragon) and bringer of light to the souls of the dead on the Last Day; at various historical times and in various cultures, a number of powers have been attributed to him including healing and the protection of cemeteries. His name is by tradition said to mean "Who is like El (God)?", which according to some commentators may have been a very early war-cry of the ancient Israelites, and millennia later he is still considered by many Jews to act as metaphysical defender of Israel.

Saladin, or Salah-ad-Din Yusuf ibn-Aiyub Kurdish Muslim (Saracen) leader in the twelfth century, renowned among his own people and among the invading crusaders for his military genius and chivalry. His major concern was always to unify the disparate Muslim factions and reconquer the Holy Land. He is remembered for his military prowess, his chivalry, and the mercy and magnanimity he showed towards the citizens and defenders of Jerusalem when he took that city and signalled the final decline of Christian power in the East.

Solomon's Temple in Jerusalem The legendary "First Temple" supposedly built by the ancient Hebrews after capturing and occupying Jerusalem, which then became the Israelites' capital; the inspiration of King David. It was allegedly built in around 966 BCE, under the direction of his son Solomon, primarily to house the Ark of the Covenant, symbolizing the "contract" between God and His Chosen People.

Sufis and Sufism Mystical movement within Islam comprising several distinct initiatory orders, which have their own rites and practices leading to greater humility and growing union with God.

Temple of Solomon *See* **Solomon's Temple**.

Teutonic Knights, the The "Brotherhood of the German House of St. Mary in Jerusalem" was founded in 1190 by German knights and priests to establish hospital care for pilgrims during the Third Crusade at the Siege of Acre; it was at Acre that the new order was based. Within 20 years, however, their purpose had changed from the protection of pilgrims to military endeavors to recapture Jerusalem. After the final defeat of the crusaders, the Teutonic Knights moved north to Prussia where they set up military rule under the guise of a monastic state, and indulged in bloody incursions into Poland and Lithuania. The Order was technically dissolved by Napoleon Bonaparte in 1809, although it still nominally exists as a charitable organization.

Torah, the The sacred "Law of Moses," contained within the first five books of the Hebrew Bible: Genesis, Exodus, Leviticus, Numbers, and Deuteronomy (the Pentateuch). The Torah scrolls are reverently housed in an "ark," or tabernacle, in every synagogue.

BIBLIOGRAPHY & FURTHER READING

BIBLIOGRAPHY

Addison, Charles G, *The History of the Knights Templar*,
    Adventures Unlimited Press, Illinois, 1997.

Allegro, John, *The Dead Sea Scrolls and the Christian Myth*,
    Prometheus Books, New York, 1992.

Anderson, William, *The Rise of the Gothic*, Hutchinson,
    London, 1986.

Armstrong, Karen, *A History of Muhammad*,
    HarperSanFrancisco, San Francisco, 1993.

Aué, Michèle, *Cathar Country*, MSM, Paris, 1995.

Baigent, Michael and Leigh, Richard, *The Inquisition*,
    Penguin, London, 2000.

Barber, Malcolm, *The Trial of the Templars*,
    Cambridge University Press, Cambridge, U.K, 2006.

Begg, Ean, *The Cult of the Black Virgin*,
    Arkana, London, 1996.

Bruno, S. T., *Templar Organization*, AuthorHouse,
    Indiana, 2000.

Burman, Edward, *The Templars: Knights of God*,
    Inner Traditions Bear and Company, Vermont, 1990.

Burman, Edward, *The Inquisition: The Hammer of Heresy*,
    Dorset Press, New York, 1994.

Costen, Michael, *The Cathars and the Albigensian Crusade*,
    Manchester University Press, Manchester, U.K, 1997.

Dafoe, Stephen & Butler, Alan, *The Warriors and the
    Bankers*, Templar Books, Ontario, 1999.

Delaporte, Y., and Houvet, E. *Les Trois Notre Dames de
    Chartres*, Paris, 1955.

Demurger, Alain, *The Last Templar*, ,
    Profile Books Ltd, London, 2005.

Gardner, Laurence, *Lost Secrets of the Sacred Ark*,
    Element Books, Dorset, U.K, 2004.

Goodwin, Godfrey, *Islamic Spain*,
    Chronicle Books, San Francisco, 2000.

Halam, Elizabeth, ed. *The Chronicles of the Crusades*,
    Welcome Rain Publishers, New York, 2001.

Hancock, Graham, *The Sign and the Seal*, Doubleday,
    New York, 1993.

Johnson, Paul, *A History of Christianity*,
    Weidenfeld & Nicholson, London, 1978.

The Lost Books of the Bible,
    Gramercy Books, New York, 1988.

Martin, S., *The Knights Templar*, Pocket Essentials,
    Manchester, U.K, 2004.

Miller, Malcolm, *Chartres Cathedral*, Pitkin Guides,
    Hampshire, UK, 1996.

Nicholson, H., *The Knights Templar, A New History*,
    Sutton Publishing Ltd, Gloucestershire, UK, 2004.

Osman, Ahmed, *Out of Egypt: Unearthing the Roots of True
    Christianity*, Century, London, 1998.

Partner, Peter, *The Knights Templar and Their Myth*,
    Inner Traditions Bear and Company, Vermont, 1990.

Read, Piers Paul, *The Templars*, Da Capo Press, MA, 2001.

Robinson, John J., *Dungeon, Fire and Sword*,
Caxton Editions, London, 2001.

Robinson, John J., *Born in blood*,
M. Evans and Company Inc, New York, 1990.

Robinson, James M., ed. *The Nag Hammadi Library
in English*, Brill, New York, 1998.

Selwood, D., *Knights of the Cloister*,
The Boydell Press, Suffolk, U.K, 2002.

Strachan, Gordon, *Chartres*, Floris Books, Edinburgh, 2003.

Upton-Ward, J.M., *The Rule of the Templars*,
Boydell Press, Suffolk, U.K, 2002.

Wallace-Murphy, Tim and Hopkins, Marilyn, *Rosslyn,
Guardian of the Secrets of the Holy Grail*,
Element Books, Dorset, U.K, 1999.

Wallace-Murphy, Tim and Hopkins, Marilyn, and Simmans,
Graham, *Rex Deus*, Element Books, Dorset, U.K, 2000.

Wallace-Murphy, Tim and Hopkins, Marilyn,
Custodians of Truth, Red Wheel Weiser, MA, 2005.

Wallace-Murphy, T, *Cracking the Symbol Code*,
Watkins Publishing, London, 2006.

Wilson, Ian, *The Turin Shroud*,
Weidenfeld & Nicholson, London, 1998.

FURTHER READING

Addison, Charles G, *The History of the Knights Templar*,
Black Books, London, 1995.

Albany, HRH Prince Michael of, *The Forgotten Monarchy
of Scotland*, Vega Books, London, 2002.

Ambelain, Robert, *Jesus ou le Mortel Sécret des Templiers*,
Robert Lafont, Paris, 1970.

Baigent, Michael and Leigh, Richard,
The Temple and the Lodge, Arrow, London, 2006.

Baigent, Michael and Leigh, Richard,
The Messianic Legacy, Henry Holt, New York, 1987.

Cannon, Dolores, *Jesus and the Essenes*,
Ozark Mountain Publishing, Arkansas, 2002.

Christie-Murray, David, *A History of Heresy*,
Oxford Paperbacks, Oxford, U.K, 1989.

DeClari, Robert, *The Conquest of Constantinople*,
trans. E. H. McNeal, Columbia University Press,
Columbia, 2005.

Ellis, Ralph, *Jesus, Last of the Pharaohs*,
Edfu Books, Cheshire, U.K, 2000.

Feather, Robert, *The Copper Scroll Decoded*,
HarperCollins, London, 2000.

Fisher, H. A. L., *A History of Europe*,
Edward Arnold & Co, London, 1936.

Gimpell, Jean, *The Cathedral Builders*, Pimlico, London, 1993.

Hamilton, Bernard, *The Albigensian Crusade*,
The Historical Association, London, 1974.

James, Bruno S., *St. Bernard of Clairvaux*,
Hodder and Stoughton, London, 1957.

Lacroix, P., *Military and Religious Life in the Middle Ages*,
Chapman & Hall, London, 1974.

Oldenburg, Zoé, *Massacre at Montségur*,
Weidenfeld & Nicholson, London, 2001.

Picknett, Lynn & Prince, Clive, *The Templar Revelation*,
Simon and Schuster Inc, New York, 1998.

Runciman, Stephen, *A History of the Crusades*,
Penguin, London, 1991.

Serrus, Georges, *The Land of the Cathars*,
Editions Loubatières, Portet-sur-Garonne, France, 1990.

INDEX

ACKNOWLEDGMENTS

PICTURE CREDITS

The publishers would like to thank the following agencies and institutions for permission to use their images. Every effort has been made to trace the copyright holder, but if there are any omissions, then please contact the publisher and the situation will be rectified.

Akg Images/British Library: 58; Jean-Paul Dumontier: 20; Erich Lessing: 16; Ullstein-Otto: 85; **Alamy**/Jack Sullivan: 78; **The Art Archive**/Dagli Orli: 60; Macerata University Le Marche Italy/Dagli Orti: 108; **The Bodleian Library, Oxford, UK:** 78; **Bridgeman Art Library**/Biblioteca Apostolica Vaticana, The Vatican, Italy: 103; Biblioteca Nazionale, Turin, Italy; Roger-Viollet, Paris: 87; Bibliothèque des Arts Decoratifs, Paris, France; Archives Charmet: 69, 109; Bibliothèque Municipale, Castres, France; Giraudon: 35; Bibliothèque Nationale, Paris, France: 66; British Library, London, UK: 51, 72, 110, 112, 62; Château de Versailles, France: 56, 70; Historisches Museum der Stadt, Vienna, Austria: 127; Collection of the Earl of Leicester, Holkham Hall, Norfolk: 29; Louvre, Paris, France: 79, 104; Musée Condé, Chantilly, France, Lauros/Giraudon: 74; Prado, Madrid, Spain: 115, 120; Private Collection: 123; Private Collection, © Heini Schneebeli: 94; Private Collection, Archives Charmet: 7, 41; Private Collection, Ken Welsh: 18; Stapleton Collection, UK: 76, 125; **Corbis**/Paul Almasy: 91; The Art Archive: 100; Bettmann: 4, 21, 38, 45, 101, 130; Gianni Dagli Orti: 43; Chris Hellier: 11; Krause Johansen/Archivo Iconografico, SA: 118; Michael Maslan Historic Photographs: 40; West Semitic Research /Dead Sea Scrolls Foundation: 10; **Barry Crouch, Essex CC**: 28; **Joan de Fuguet:** 122; **Getty Images**/Hulton Archive: 5, 26, 137; **Grand Lodge of Scotland:** 124; **Lorraine Harrison:** 14, 17, 42, 44, 57; **iStockphoto**/Adrian Hughes: 107; Bart Parren: 86; **Library and Museum of Freemasonry:** 126; **Lodge Temple:** 128; **Mary Evans Picture Library:** 113; **Ian Potts:** 52, 55; **Denys Pringle:** 30, 73, 106; **Antonia Reeve:** 99; **Topfoto:** 98; The Master and Fellows of Corpus Christi College, Cambridge: 53; Fortean: 75, 116; Fotomas: 8, 82; HIP/The British Library: 12, 23, 48, 50, 65; Topham Picturepoint: 31, 68; Roger Viollet: 3, 15, 37, 47, 97; **Tim Wallace-Murphy:** 4, 32, 83, 84, 89, 95, 96, 99; © Clive Hicks: 34; © Patrick Keene: 88.

FRONT COVER: **Bridgeman Art Library**/Bibliothèque des Arts Decoratifs, Paris, France, Archives Charmet.

AUTHOR ACKNOWLEDGMENTS

My thanks go to David Alexander, without whom this work would not have come to fruition, and to Hazel Songhurst and the editorial team at Ivy Press for their part in finding the illustrations and bringing this book together. I am particularly grateful to my friend and housemate, Raine, who kept me supplied with endless cups of tea while the work was in progress, and to Tim Wallace-Murphy for his help and guidance over the last twelve years.